Background Subtraction

Theory and Practice

Synthesis Lectures on Computer Vision

Editor

Gérard Medioni, *University of Southern California*
Sven Dickinson, *University of Toronto*

Synthesis Lectures on Computer Vision is edited by Gérard Medioni of the University of Southern California and Sven Dickinson of the University of Toronto. The series publishes 50- to 150 page publications on topics pertaining to computer vision and pattern recognition.

Background Subtraction: Theory and Practice
Ahmed Elgammal

ISBN: 978-3-031-00685-2   paperback
ISBN: 978-3-031-01813-8   ebook

DOI 10.1007/978-3-031-01813-8

A Publication in the Springer series
SYNTHESIS LECTURES ON COMPUTER VISION

Lecture #6
Series Editors: Gérard Medioni, *University of Southern California*
                Sven Dickinson, *University of Toronto*
Series ISSN
Print 2153-1056   Electronic 2153-1064

Background Subtraction

Theory and Practice

Ahmed Elgammal
Rutgers University

SYNTHESIS LECTURES ON COMPUTER VISION #6

ABSTRACT

Background subtraction is a widely used concept for detection of moving objects in videos. In the last two decades there has been a lot of development in designing algorithms for background subtraction, as well as wide use of these algorithms in various important applications, such as visual surveillance, sports video analysis, motion capture, etc. Various statistical approaches have been proposed to model scene backgrounds. The concept of background subtraction also has been extended to detect objects from videos captured from moving cameras. This book reviews the concept and practice of background subtraction. We discuss several traditional statistical background subtraction models, including the widely used parametric Gaussian mixture models and non-parametric models. We also discuss the issue of shadow suppression, which is essential for human motion analysis applications. This book discusses approaches and tradeoffs for background maintenance. This book also reviews many of the recent developments in background subtraction paradigm. Recent advances in developing algorithms for background subtraction from moving cameras are described, including motion-compensation-based approaches and motion-segmentation-based approaches.

For links to the videos to accompany this book, please see
https://sites.google.com/a/morganclaypool.com/backgroundsubtraction/.

KEYWORDS

background subtraction, segmentation, visual surveillance, gaussian mixture model, kernel density estimation, moving object detection, shadow detection, figure-ground segmentation, motion segmentation, motion compensation, layered scene segmentation

To my wife for her emotional support,
to my parents for all what they have given me,
and to my kids for the joy they bring to my life.

— Ahmed

Contents

Preface

With cameras around us everywhere, a continuos stream of a vast amount of videos comes that need to be processed and analyzed. This explosion of videos drives the research and development in the computer vision community at large. The detection of foreground objects is the first step in several computer vision processing pipelines. The are several solution paradigms for detecting foreground objects in videos, with varying assumptions depending on the type of imaging sensor, the motion of the imaging platform, whether the video is available online or offline, and the characteristics of the applications. Among these solutions comes *Background Subtraction* as one of the widely used paradigms to detect foreground regions in videos. The success of Background Subtraction algorithms led to the development of the camera-based automated surveillance industry, as well several video analysis applications such as sports analysis, event detection, activity recognition, marker-less motion capture systems, and others.

The Background Subtraction paradigm has an over two-decades history in the computer vision field, with roots in image processing and even deeper roots extending to the earlier years of photography. With over 500 papers published in conferences, workshops, and journals related to background subtraction, it is very hard for a student to get hold of the different developments in this area, and put them in the right historical perspective. The goal of this book is to give the reader a birds-eye view of this topic, with enough details about the major approaches developed over the last two decades, without overwhelming the reader with all variants of these approaches. This book is not intended to be a comprehensive survey of every paper on the subject, but rather a gentle guide to exploring the topic.

This book is organized in three chapters. Chapter 1 introduces the problem of foreground detection in videos and explores solutions ranging from foreground detectors, motion segmentation, and video segmentation to background subtraction. The goal is to highlight the basic assumptions behind each of these paradigms and shed light on where background subtraction fits within the big picture. Chapter 2 reviews some of the traditional statistical background models, including parametric and non-parametric models, which are the bases for many algorithms for background subtraction. Chapter 2 also discusses issues related to detecting shadows and maintaining the background representation. Chapter 3 discusses the extensions of background subtraction to deal with videos captured from moving cameras. The chapter describes motion-compensation-based approaches, layered-motion segmentation, and motion-segmentation-based approaches for background subtraction from a moving platform.

Ahmed Elgammal
November 2014

Acknowledgments

I would like to thank Gérard Medioni and Sven Dickinson, the editors of this "Synthesis Lectures on Computer Vision" series for giving me this opportunity to serve the community by writing this book. I would like to thank Ali Elqursh for helping with some of the materials in Chapter 3. I greatly appreciate the help of the editor of the series, Diane Cerra. I would like to thank the researchers who granted me permission to use figures from their papers in this book, including: Edward H. Adelson, Thanarat H. Chalidabhongse, Bohyung Han, Ivan Huerta, Kyungnam Kim, Anurag Mittal, Yaser Sheikh, and Jürgen Stauder.

Ahmed Elgammal
November 2014

Figure Credits

Figure 2.1	From Guéziec, A. Tracking pitches for broadcast television. *Computer*, 35(3):38–43. Copyright © 2002, IEEE. DOI: 10.1109/2.989928. Used with permission.
Figures 2.2, 2.5, 2.9	From Elgammal, et al. Nonparametric background model for background subtraction. In *ECCV '00 Proceedings of the 6th European Conference on Computer Vision-Part II*: Pages 751–767. Copyright © 2000, Springer-Verlag London, UK. ISBN: 3-540-67686-4. Used with permission.
Figures 2.3, 2.14	Based on Elgammal, et al. Nonparametric background model for background subtraction. In *ECCV '00 Proceedings of the 6th European Conference on Computer Vision-Part II*: Pages 751–767. Copyright © 2000, Springer-Verlag London, UK. ISBN: 3-540-67686-4.
Figure 2.8	Based on Stauder, et al. Detection of moving cast shadows for object segmentation. *IEEE Transactions on Multimedia*, (Volume: 1, Issue: 1), page(s): 65–76. Copyright © 1999, IEEE. DOI: 10.1109/6046.748172. Courtesy of Jürgen Stauder.
Figure 2.10	Based on Horprasert, et al. (2000). A robust background subtraction and shadow detection. In *Proceedings of the 4th Asian Conference on Computer Vision*, pages 983–988. Courtesy of Thanarat Horprasert.
Figure 2.11	Based on Huerta, et al. Detection and removal of chromatic moving shadows in surveillance scenarios. *2009 IEEE 12th International Conference on Computer Vision*, pages 1499–1506. Copyright © 2009, IEEE. DOI: 10.1109/ICCV.2009.5459280. Courtesy of Ivan Huerta.
Figure 2.12	From Horprasert, et al. A robust background subtraction and shadow detection. In *Lecture Notes in Computer Science*: *Proceedings of the 4th Asian Conference on Computer Vision*, pages 983–988. Copyright © 2000, Springer Heidelberg Dordrecht London New York. Used with permission.

Figure 2.13   From Huerta, et al. Detection and removal of chromatic moving shadows in surveillance scenarios. *2009 IEEE 12th International Conference on Computer Vision*, pages 1499–1506. Copyright © 2009, IEEE. DOI: 10.1109/ICCV.2009.5459280. Used with permission.

Figure 2.15   Based on Kim, et al. Background updating for visual surveillance. *Advances in Visual Computing: First International Symposium, ISVC 2005*, Lake Tahoe, NV, USA, December 5-7, 2005. Copyright © 2005, Springer Berlin Heidelberg. DOI: 10.1007/11595755_41. Courtesy of Kyungnam Kim.

Figure 3.1   From Mittal, A. and Huttenlocher, D. Scene modeling for wide area surveillance and image synthesis. *IEEE Conference on Computer Vision and Pattern Recognition, 2000: Proceedings*. Copyright © 2000, IEEE. DOI: 10.1109/CVPR.2000.854767. Used with permission.

Figure 3.2   Based on Wang, J. and Adelson, E. Representing Moving Images with Layers. *IEEE Transactions on Image Processing* (Volume: 3, Issue: 5). Copyright © 1994, IEEE. DOI: 10.1109/83.334981. Courtesy of Edward H. Adelson.

Figure 3.3   Based on Sheikh, et al. Background Subtraction for Freely Moving Cameras. *2009 IEEE 12th International Conference on Computer Vision*. Copyright © 2009, IEEE. DOI: 10.1109/ICCV.2009.5459334. Courtesy of Yaser Sheikh.

Figure 3.4   Based on Kwak, et al. Generalized Background Subtraction Based on Hybrid Inference by Belief Propagation and Bayesian Filtering. *2011 IEEE International Conference on Computer Vision (ICCV)*. Copyright © 2011, IEEE. DOI: 10.1109/ICCV.2011.6126494. Courtesy of Bohyung Han.

Figures 3.5, 3.6, 3.7   From Elqursh, A. and Elgammal, A. Online moving camera background subtraction. *Computer Vision – ECCV 2012: 12th European Conference on Computer Vision, Florence, Italy, October 7-13, 2012, Proceedings, Part VI*. Copyright © 2012, Springer-Verlag Berlin Heidelberg. DOI: 10.1007/978-3-642-33783-3_17. Used with permission.

CHAPTER 1

Object Detection and Segmentation in Videos

1.1 CHARACTERIZATION OF VIDEO DATA

Cameras are everywhere nowadays—in everyone's cell phone, at every traffic intersection, on the ceilings and walls of every store, mall, airport, subway, stadium etc. Cameras are watching us constantly at different scale: satellite cameras at a large scale; surveillance cameras at a street-scene scale; and even inside our bodies internal-body cameras are monitoring us at a micro scale. With all these camera sensors available comes a huge amount of digital video data. It is quite difficult to get an estimate of the amounts of images and videos captured every day. However, we can get some indication by looking at the statistics from some popular websites. In 2009, it was estimated that 2.5 billion photos were uploaded to Facebook every month—that is 30 billion photos per year on Facebook alone. This number keeps monotonically increasing.[1] In 2012, it was estimated that there is about 7 petabyte ($1024^4 byte \approx 10^{15} byte$) of photo content uploaded to Facebook every month. In terms of videos, according to YouTube Statistics in 2014,[2] the number of hours of videos being uploaded every minute is monotonically increasing from 35 hr/min in 2010, to 48 hr/min in 2011, to 72 hr/min in 2013, to 100 hr/min in 2014. This remains just a small fraction compared to videos captured daily by millions of surveillance cameras everywhere.

With that continuous increase in the volume of video data being captured every day comes the opportunity and the need for various real-world applications that require high-level recognition of objects, scenes, activities, and events in video data. Examples of these applications include automated visual surveillance, video archival and retrieval, autonomous driving, sports analysis, marker-less motion capture, etc. The detection and segmentation of objects of interest, such as humans and vehicles, are the first stages in such automated visual event-detection applications. It is always desirable to achieve a very high accuracy in the detection of targets with the lowest-possible false alarm rates.

We can characterize the domains of videos across two orthogonal dimensions: camera motion (videos captured from a static camera vs. mobile platform); and the processing requirement for decision-making (offline videos vs. online streaming videos). This results in four different categories of videos, as shown in Figure 1.1. In the last three decades, several algorithms have been developed to address the detection and segmentation of objects of interest, capitalizing on the

---

[1] The figures for Facebook data are according to `royal.pingdom.com` Internet in numbers blog.
[2] YouTube statistics `https://www.youtube.com/yt/press/statistics.html` accessed in July 2014.

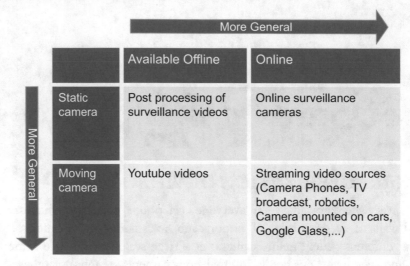

Figure 1.1: Classification of the different types of videos based on the camera motion and processing needs.

characteristics of each of these categories of videos to achieve specialized effective and efficient solutions for them.

The distinction between offline videos and online streaming videos is essential. In many applications, online real-time processing is needed to support decision-making, for example, for robotic navigation. In other applications, the videos are available offline, e.g., Youtube videos, and offline processing can be afforded. The distinction between online vs. offline processing is not mainly about the real-time performance constraint. Processing online videos is far more challenging than processing offline videos, since, at any point of time in an online video, the future frames are not available. This makes it hard to distinguish between objects that move coherently up to the current frame, but then start to move independently in future frames. Therefore, most motion-segmentation algorithms rely on the availability of the video offline.

In visual surveillance applications, stationary cameras or pan-tilt-zoom (PTZ) cameras are used to monitor activities at outdoor or indoor sites. In some surveillance applications, online real-time processing of videos is needed, while in other applications, videos are compressed and recorded and processing is done offline. Since the cameras are stationary, the detection of moving objects can be achieved by comparing each new frame with a representation of the scene background. This process is called *background subtraction* and the scene representation is called the *background model*. The scene here is assumed to be stationary or quasi stationary. Figure 1.2 illustrates a block diagram of a typical background subtraction process. Whether processing is needed online or offline for this type of videos, traditional background subtraction techniques provide

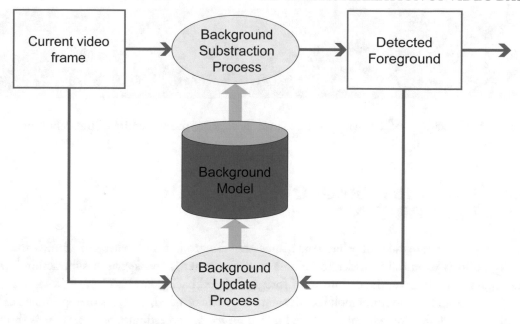

Figure 1.2: Block diagram of the background subtraction process.

effective solutions for the detection and segmentation of targets in these scenarios. We provide an overview of these traditional techniques in Chapter 2.

However, most of today's videos are captured from moving platforms (camera phones, cameras mounted on ground vehicles, drones, robots, soldiers, etc.) Traditional background subtraction algorithms are not applicable for the moving-camera case. There have been some extensions of background subtraction algorithms to deal with mobile cameras where camera motion is known or scene geometry is restricted, such as stationary mounted pan-tilt-zoom cameras, or videos captured from high altitudes (e.g., drones). Such extensions utilize motion compensation to generalize background subtraction to such videos. We review these extensions in Section 3.2. There have been also some recent algorithms developed to generalize the concept of background subtraction dealing with freely moving cameras (we review such algorithms in Section 3.5). In contrast to background subtraction approaches, there are other solutions for the detection and segmentation of objects in videos, which do not assume stationarity of the camera. These solutions include object detectors, video segmentation, and motion segmentation approaches. We briefly review possible solutions for detecting objects in videos in Section 1.3.

Figure 1.3: Example of a moving-camera video illustrating the ambiguity of the definition of fore-ground/background.

1.2   WHAT IS FOREGROUND AND WHAT IS BACKGROUND?

Answering the question of what constitutes the foreground and what constitutes the scene background is essential in order to be able to define what is "background subtraction." In the stationary-camera case, the definition of foreground and background is clear—a foreground object is anything that does not look like the stationary background, in terms of appearance or local motion. This definition assumes that we know *a priori*, or can estimate online, what is the scene background. Therefore, it suffices to model the statistical distribution of the scene background features, and detecting the foreground is mainly a process of detecting outliers to that distribution. An alternative definition in the case of a stationary camera and scene is: any "significantly" moving object is foreground, while any stationary object is part of the scene background. Obviously, the above two definitions are not equivalent.

In the case of a freely moving camera, the definition of foreground and background is ambiguous. For example, let us consider the frames in Figure 1.3, taken from a video captured by a moving camera. What is the foreground and what is the background in this case? Should the tree be considered the foreground? If we have a way to recover the depth information, and if we are interested in objects that are closer to the camera, then we might consider the tree as foreground. However, relying on depth is also ambiguous. What is the threshold on depth that we can use to decide about the foreground? What about the ground plan, for example, where the depth changes smoothly? If we consider motion rather than depth, the answer is not clear either. Considering apparent image motion (2D motion), every thing in the scene is moving. Considering the physical motion (recovering 3D motion), the tree, the ground, and the building all constitute one rigid entity that has the same motion.

The problem of figure/ground separation is well studied in the psychology of vision. Results of such studies have highly influenced the field of perceptual grouping in computer vision. In the case of a single image, the definition of figure/ground can be quite ambiguous. Among the most important factors psychology studies pointed out, to determine figure/ground are: surroundness (a region that is completely surrounded by another); size (smaller regions are perceived as figures); orientation (vertical and horizontal regions are perceived more frequently as figures); contrast (the region with greatest contrast to its surrounding is perceived as a figure); symmetry, convexity, and parallelism of the contour. Such low-level cues have been widely used in figure/ground segmentation literature and in salient region detection.

Higher-level cues are quite important as well; figure/ground processing is highly influenced by knowledge of specific object shapes. Peterson and Gibson [1991] experiments clearly gave evidence to the role of familiar shapes in figure/ground processing. However, it is not clear whether figure/ground organization precedes object recognition and later recognition process gives feedback to the figure/ground process, or there exists prefigural recognition process before any figure/ground decision. In both cases it is clear that figure/ground separation is a process that is intertwined with recognition. This issue received attention in the computer vision community as well as through many recent papers that use shape priors in segmentation.

Dynamic figure/ground processing seems to be far less ambiguous compared to single image figure/ground processing. It is clear from psychological experiments that common fate (the tendency to group tokens that move with the same direction and speed) plays a significant role in perceptual grouping and figure/ground separation in dynamic scenes. The concept of common fate can be generalized to include any kind of rigid motion and also configural [Johansson, 1950] and biological motion [Johansson, 1973].

1.3   THE SPACE OF SOLUTIONS

This section describes the main alternative paradigms for object detection and segmentation in videos. We contrast these paradigms and highlight their capabilities and limitations.

1.3.1   FOREGROUND DETECTION VS. BACKGROUND SUBTRACTION

In the last decade, many object-specific "foreground-detection" algorithms have been introduced. Detecting objects of interest can be achieved through designing and learning about specialized detectors using large training data, e.g., pedestrian detector, face detector, vehicle detector, bicycle detector, etc. Given a trained classifier for the object, the occurrences of that object in the image are found by exhaustively scanning the image and applying the detector at each location and scale. This concept has been successfully used in detecting pedestrians and vehicles in images [Dalal and Triggs, 2005, Gavrila, 2000, Oren et al., 1997, e.g.]. Also, this concept is widely used for face detection [Viola and Jones, 2004]. These algorithms work best when the object has limited appearance variability, for example for pedestrian detection, however it is very hard to train these detectors for various human poses, variations in shape, and appearances that are expected to appear in unconstrained videos. Also, these algorithms are hard to scale to detect a large number of objects of interest with desired accuracy/false alarm rates. Recent advances in deep convolutional network architecture made it possible to build detectors for 1,000 categories [Sermanet et al., 2013], however, with limited precision. Alternatively, feature-based/part-based detectors can accommodate large variability of object poses and within-class variability. In such approaches, candidate object parts are detected and geometric constrains are used on these parts to detect objects. For example pictorial structure-based models can deal with large within-class variability in human poses [Felzenszwalb and Huttenlocher, 2005, Felzenszwalb et al., 2010]

Table 1.1: A comparison between background subtraction and foreground detection approaches

	Background Subtraction	Foreground Object Detector
Assumption about camera motion	Stationary Camera [†]	No assumption
Output	Accurate Segmentation of objects	Bounding Boxes [‡]
Detected Objects	Any non-background object	Object-specific detector
Training	Needs bootstrapping for few seconds	Needs offline training
Handling Videos	Designed for detection from video	Designed for single-image detection
Performance	Realtime	Realtime

[†] This does not include recent approaches for background subtraction from a moving camera

[‡] Post processing of the bounding box can provide a segmentation of the object

For the case of static-camera videos, object-specific detectors are far from matching the performance of a typical background-subtraction algorithm, in terms of false positives or false negatives, and moreover, they do not provide exact segmentation of objects, but rather a bounding box(s) around the object and its parts. To the contrary, for the case of mobile-camera videos, object-specific foreground-detection algorithms are directly applicable, as they can be applied to every frame in the video, since they do not assume stationary camera or scene.

However, despite providing an applicable solution, there are three fundamental limitations to these algorithms that make them not effective in dealing with videos. First, these algorithms are designed to detect objects from images, and hence, do not utilize any temporal constraints in the video. Second, even in images, the performance of these algorithms is far from being readily useful in real-world applications. Results of the Pascal Challenge 2011 showed that the best-achieved precision for detecting people and cars is 51.6% and 54.5% respectively. The performance degrades significantly if the targets are smaller in size or occluded. A recent evaluation on a challenging face dataset showed that state-of-the-art face-detection algorithms could only achieve 70% accuracy with more than 1 FPPI (false positive per image) [Jain and Learned-Miller, 2011]. A recent evaluation of state-of-the-art pedestrian-detection algorithms found that such algorithms have a recall of no more than 60% for un-occluded pedestrians with 80-pixel height at a 1 FPPI (false positive per image) [Dollár et al., 2009]. The performance of state-of-the-art and widely used deformable part models is 33% and 43% (precision) for detecting cars and people respectively, evaluated on the PASCAL VOC 2008 dataset [Felzenszwalb et al., 2010]. Also, scaling these algorithms for a large number of classes is challenging, since they require training for each object category. At run time, a detector for each object class needs to be used. Recently, Dean et al. [2013] show how part-based models can be scaled up for detecting 100K classes efficiently, however, the accuracy reported on PASCAL VOC 2007 dataset is limited to 24% precision. The state-of-the-art for deep neural-network-detection models on the ImageNet ILSVRC 2013 competition is also on the same range of precision [Sermanet et al., 2013].

Table 1.1 provides a rough comparison of the two paradigms (background subtraction vs. object-specific detectors). Typically, these two paradigms are not comparable since they are designed for different tasks (segmentation of videos vs. detection in images). However, this comparison is useful to highlight that object-specific detectors do not provide an effective solution to deal with object detection in videos, in the same caliber that traditional background-subtraction algorithms offer.

1.3.2   VIDEO SEGMENTATION AND MOTION SEGMENTATION

Video segmentation generalizes the concept of image segmentation, and attempts to group pixels into spatiotemporal regions that exhibit coherency in both appearance and motion. Several existing approaches for video segmentation cluster the pixels over the whole video or over temporal sliding windows. First, multidimensional features are extracted representing photometric and motion properties. Then, clustering is used to gather evidence of pixel groupings in the feature space. Such clustering can be done using Gaussian mixture models [Greenspan et al., 2002], mean-shift [DeMenthon and Megret, 2002, Wang et al., 2004], and spectral clustering [Fowlkes et al., 2004]. However, it is unclear how to use the resulting segmented regions for detecting objects of interest in video. In practice, one can identify objects that move coherently but are composed of multiple regions with different appearances. Similarly, articulated objects may be formed of multiple regions of different motions with common appearances. Typically, a video-segmentation technique produces an over-segmentation of such objects.

Whereas objects can be composed of different parts with different appearances, they typically move as a coherent region. Therefore, one can argue that, by segmenting differently moving objects in the scene, one can easily detect objects of interest in the scene. Traditionally, object detection in a video sequence has been formulated as detecting outliers to dominant apparent image motion between two frames, e.g., [Irani and Anandan, 1998, Irani et al., 1994, Odobez and Bouthemy, 1997]; such approaches assume that objects are relatively small compared to the scene. However, there exist several challenges with formulating the detection problem as a motion-segmentation problem. The observed image motion is the result of the perspective projection of the 3D motion. Thus, the straightforward approach of segmenting based on translational motion over two frames typically leads to poor results. On the other hand, using richer models, such as affine camera motion, can only segment a very small subset of pixels—namely those that can be tracked through the entire frame sequence. Furthermore, many methods make the assumption that objects are rigid, and, as a consequence, over-segment articulated and non-rigid objects. For all those reasons, motion segmentation is still an active area of research.

1.4   BACKGROUND SUBTRACTION CONCEPT

The above discussion highlights the fact that, despite that there are applicable solutions for detecting objects in videos, these solutions are far from being effective. The goal of the research in the area of background subtraction is to develop efficient and effective algorithms for detecting and segmenting the foreground regions in videos. What distinguishes background subtraction algorithms in general from all other detection and segmentation algorithms is that they maintain a representation of the scene background, and use this representation to help detect the foreground objects. In this book, we do not restrict the term "background subtraction" to the traditional static-camera case. Instead, we highlight algorithms that are applicable for stationary cameras, as well as moving cameras. In that sense, the diagram in Figure 1.2 serves as a general block diagram to all algorithms belonging to the background-subtraction paradigm.

The concept of background modeling is rooted in the early days of photography in the fist half of the 19th century, where it was typical to expose film for an extended period of time, leading to the capture of the scene background without fast-moving objects. The use of a background-subtraction process to detect moving objects was originated in image analysis and emanated from the concept of change detection, a process in which two images of the same scene, taken at different time instances, are compared, for example, in Landsat Imagery, e.g., [Eghbali, 1979, Jain and Nagel, 1979]. Today, background subtraction is a concept widely used to detect moving objects in videos taken from a static camera, and even extends to videos taken from moving cameras. In the last two decades, several algorithms have been developed for background subtraction and were used in various important applications, such as visual surveillance, sports video analysis, motion capture, etc.

CHAPTER 2

Background Subtraction from a Stationary Camera

Background subtraction is a widely used concept to detect moving objects in videos taken from a static camera. In the last two decades, several algorithms have been developed for background subtraction and were used in various important applications such as visual surveillance, analysis of sports video, marker-less motion capture, etc. Various statistical approaches have been proposed to model scene background. In this chapter we review the concept and practice background subtraction. We discuss several basic statistical background-subtraction models, including parametric Gaussian models and non-parametric models. We discuss the issue of shadow suppression, which is essential for human motion analysis applications. We also discuss approaches and tradeoffs for background maintenance. We also point out many of the recent developments in background-subtraction paradigms. The organization of this chapter is as follows. Section 2.1 introduces the concept and history of background models. Section 2.2 discusses some of the challenges in building a background model for detection. Sections 2.3, 2.4, and 2.5–2.7 discuss some of the basic and widely used background modeling techniques. Section 2.8 discusses how to deal with color information to avoid detecting shadows. Section 2.9 highlights the tradeoffs and challenges in updating background models.

2.1 INTRODUCTION

In visual-surveillance applications, stationary cameras or pan-tilt-zoom (PTZ) cameras are used to monitor activities at outdoor or indoor sites. Since the camera is stationary, the detection of moving objects can be achieved by comparing each new frame with a representation of the scene background. This process is called *background subtraction* and the scene representation is called the *background model*. The scene here is assumed to be stationary or quasi stationary.

Typically, the background-subtraction process forms the first stage in automated visual surveillance systems as well as in other applications, such as motion capture, sport analysis, etc. Results from this process are used for further processing, such as tracking targets and understanding events. One main advantage of target detection using background subtraction is that the outcome is an accurate segmentation of the foreground regions from the scene background. For human subjects, the process gives accurate silhouettes of the human body, which can be further used for tracking, fitting body limbs, pose and posture estimation, etc. This is in contrast to classifier-based object-based detectors, which mainly decide whether a bounding box or a region

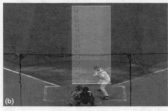

Figure 2.1: Example of an early industrial application of background subtraction. The K Zone: system developed by Sportvision for ESPN [Guéziec, 2002]. The system used a non-parametric background-subtraction algorithm [Elgammal et al., 2000] for the detection of the baseball, and Kalman Filter [Kalman, 1960] for tracking. The system could detect and track the ball in real time. The system was used by ESPN for its Major League Baseball broadcasts in 2001. Images from Guéziec, André "Tracking Pitches for Broadcast Television" [Guéziec, 2002] (IEEE ©2002).

in the image contains the object of interest or not, e.g., pedestrian detectors [Dalal and Triggs, 2005]. A detailed discussion about the contrast between these two paradigms was presented earlier, in Section 1.3.1.

The concept of background subtraction has been widely used since the early human motion analysis systems such as Pfinder [Wern et al., 1997], W4 [Haritaoglu et al., 1998], etc. Efficient and more sophisticated background-subtraction algorithms that can address challenging situations have been developed since then. The success of these algorithms led to the growth of the automated visual-surveillance industry, as well as many commercial applications, for example sports monitoring. Figure 2.1 shows an example of an early application of background subtraction in sports analysis. This system was used for real-time tracking of baseball in the ESPN Major League Baseball broadcasts in 2001 [Guéziec, 2002].

2.2   CHALLENGES IN SCENE MODELING

In any indoor or outdoor scene there are changes that occur over time. It is important for any background model to be able to tolerate these changes, either by being invariant to them or by adapting to them. These changes can be local, affecting only parts of the background, or global, affecting the entire background. The study of these changes is essential to understanding the motivations behind different background-subtraction techniques. Toyama et al. [1999] identified a list of ten challenges that a background model has to overcome, and denoted them by: *Moved objects, Time of day, Light switch, Waving trees, Camouflage, Bootstrapping, Foreground aperture, Sleeping person, Walking person, Shadows*. We can classify the possible changes in a scene background according to their source:

Figure 2.2: Illustration of the effect of small camera displacement on the result of a typical background subtraction-algorithm. From Elgammal et al. [2000] "Non-parameteric Model for Background Subtraction" (Springer ©2000).

Illumination changes:

- Gradual change in illumination, as might occur in outdoor scenes due to the change in the relative location of the sun during the day.

- Sudden change in illumination as might occur in an indoor environment by switching the lights on or off, or in an outdoor environment, e.g., a change between cloudy and sunny conditions.

- Shadows cast on the background by objects in the background itself (e.g., buildings and trees) or by moving foreground objects, i.e., moving shadows.

Motion changes:

- Global image motion due to small camera displacements. Despite the assumption that cameras are stationary, small camera displacements are common in outdoor situations due to wind load or other sources of motion, which causes global motion in the images. This causes false detections all over the image in a typical background-subtraction algorithm, as illustrated in Fig 2.2

- Motion in parts of the background. For example, tree branches moving with the wind, or rippling water. This kind of background motion causes the pixel intensity values to vary significantly with time, for example see Figure 2.3.

Structural Changes:

- These are changes introduced to the background, including any change in the geometry or the appearance of the background of the scene introduced by targets. Such changes typically occur when something relatively permanent is introduced into the scene background. For example, if somebody moves (introduces) something from (to) the background, or if a car is parked in the scene or moves out of the scene, or if a person stays stationary in the scene for an extended period, etc. Toyama et al. [1999] denoted these situations by "Moved Objects," "Sleeping Person," and "Walking Person" scenarios.

A central issue in building a representation for the scene background is the choice of the statistical model that explains the observation at a given pixel or region in the scene. The choice of the proper model depends on the type of changes expected in the scene background. Such a choice highly affects the accuracy of the detection. All the aforementioned changes affect the intensity of each pixel in the scene. The distribution of the intensity of a given pixel over time can be very wide because of aforementioned changes. For example, Figure 2.3 shows the intensity of a pixel from a typical outdoor scene over a short period of time (900 frames–30 sec). The figure also shows the intensity histogram for this pixel, which shows a wide multi-modal distribution spanning. It is clear that intensity distribution is multi-modal spanning half of the intensity range (0–255). The bottom-right of the figure shows nine histograms of the same pixel, obtained by dividing the original time interval into nine equal-length subintervals, each containing 100 frames ($3\frac{1}{3}$ sec). Looking at the intensity histograms over these partial temporal windows, we can notice that the distribution is changing significantly. All these variations occur in a very short period of time (30 sec). This figure illustrates a fundamental trade-off that faces any background-modeling algorithm. If the background model trains over a long period of time and/or adapts too slowly to changes in the scene, then we will construct a very wide and inaccurate model that will have low detection sensitivity. On the other hand, if the model adapts too quickly, this will lead to two problems: the model may adapt to the targets themselves, as their speed cannot be neglected with respect to the background variations; and it leads to an inaccurate estimation of the model parameters.

Section 2.3 discusses some of the statistical models that are widely used in background-modeling contexts. Another fundamental issue in building a background representation is what features to use for this representation or, in other words, what to model in the background. In the literature, a variety of features have been used for background modeling, including pixel-based features (pixel intensity, edges, disparity) and region-based features (e.g., image blocks). The choice of the features affects how the background model will tolerate the changes in the scene and the granularity of the detected foreground objects. Beyond choosing the statistical model and suitable features, maintaining the background representation is another challenging issue that we will discuss in Section 2.9.

In following sections we will discuss some of the existing and widely used statistical background-modeling approaches. For each model, we will discuss how the model is initialized

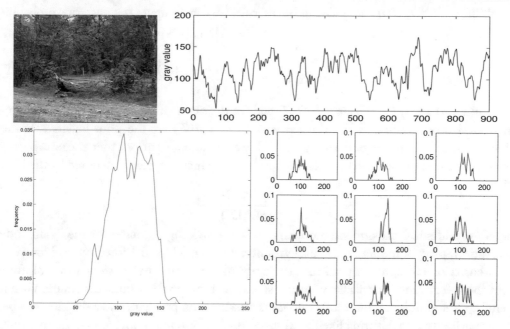

Figure 2.3: Illustration of the large variation in the intensity of a pixel in a typical outdoor scene. Top left: An outdoor scene with a circle at the top-left corner showing the location of a sample pixel. Top right: Intensity value overtime of the sample pixel, over 30 sec. Bottom left: Histogram of intensity values over the whole time period. Bottom right: Partial histograms over $3\frac{1}{3}$ second time windows. From Elgammal et al. [2000] "Non-Parameteric Model for Background Subtraction" (Springer ©2000).

and how it is maintained. For simplicity of the discussion, we will use pixel intensity as the observation. Instead, color or any other features can be used.

2.3   PROBABILISTIC BACKGROUND MODELING

The process of background/foreground segmentation can be formulated as followed: At the pixel level, the observed intensity is assumed to be a random variable that takes a value based on whether the pixel belongs to the background or the foreground. Given the intensity observed at a pixel at time t, denoted by x_t, we need to classify that pixel to either the background $\mathcal{B}$ or foreground classes $\mathcal{F}$. This is a two-class classification problem. In a Bayesian setting, we can decide whether that pixel belongs to the background or the foreground, based on the ratio between the posterior probabilities $p(\mathcal{B}|x_t)/p(\mathcal{F}|x_t)$. Using Bayes' rule, we can compute the posterior probability as

$$
\begin{aligned}
p(\mathcal{B}|x_t) &= \frac{p(x_t|\mathcal{B}) \cdot p(\mathcal{B})}{p(x_t)}, \\
p(\mathcal{F}|x_t) &= \frac{p(x_t|\mathcal{F}) \cdot p(\mathcal{F})}{p(x_t)},
\end{aligned}
$$

where $p(x_t|\mathcal{B})$ and $p(x_t|\mathcal{F})$ are the likelihoods of the observation x_t, given the background and foreground models respectively. The terms $p(\mathcal{B})$ and $p(\mathcal{F})$ are the prior beliefs that the pixel belongs to the background or the foreground. If we assume equal priors, then the ratio between the posterior reduces to the ratio between the likelihood, which is typically denoted by the likelihood ratio

$$
\frac{p(x_t|\mathcal{B})}{p(x_t|\mathcal{F})}.
$$

Therefore, statistical background modeling aims at providing estimates for the likelihood of the observation, given a model for the background and a model for the foreground. However, since the intensity of a foreground pixel can arbitrarily take any value, unless some further information about the foreground is available, we can just assume that the foreground distribution is uniform. Therefore, the problem reduces to a one-class classification problem, and a decision can be made by comparing the observation likelihood given the background model ($p(x_t|\mathcal{B})$) to a threshold, i.e.,

$$
\begin{aligned}
x_t \text{ belongs to } \mathcal{B} &\quad \text{if } p(x_t|\mathcal{B}) \geq \text{ threshold} \\
x_t \text{ belongs to } \mathcal{F} &\quad \text{otherwise.}
\end{aligned}
\tag{2.1}
$$

Therefore, any background-subtraction approach needs a statistical model to estimate the likelihood of the observation, given the background class, i.e., $p(x_t|\mathcal{B})$, which can be achieved if a history of background observations are available at that pixel. If the history observations are not purely coming from the background, i.e., foreground objects are present in the scene, the problem becomes more challenging. Statistical background models differs in the way this likelihood is estimated, based on the underlying statistical model that is used. In what follows, we will discuss parametric methods that assume a Gaussian models or a mixture of Gaussian model for the pixel process. We also will discuss non-parametric methods that do not assume a specific model for the pixel process. Coupled with the choice of the statistical model is the mechanism that the model will adapt to the scene changes. Any background-subtraction approach also has to provide a mechanism to choose the threshold (decision boundary) used in the Background/Foreground decision.

2.4   PARAMETRIC BACKGROUND MODELS

2.4.1   A SINGLE GAUSSIAN BACKGROUND MODEL

Pixel intensity is the most commonly used feature in background modeling. In a static scene, a simple noise model that can be used for the pixel process is the independent stationary additive

Gaussian noise model. In that model, the observed intensity (x_t), at a given pixel, is the sum of a constant latent intensity (μ) and white Gaussian noise,

$$x_t = \mu + \epsilon.$$

The noise distribution at a given pixel is a zero mean Gaussian distribution, $\epsilon \sim \mathcal{N}(0, \sigma^2)$. It follows that the observed intensity at that pixel is a random variable with a Gaussian distribution, i.e.,

$$P(x_t|\mathcal{B}) \approx \mathcal{N}(\mu, \sigma^2) = \frac{1}{\sigma\sqrt{2\pi}}e^{\frac{(x_t-\mu)^2}{2\sigma^2}}.$$

This Gaussian distribution model for the intensity value of a pixel is the underlying model for many background-subtraction techniques and widely know as a single Gaussian background model.

Therefore, learning the background model reduces to estimating the sample mean $\hat{\mu}$ and variance $\hat{\sigma}^2$ from history observations at each pixel. The background subtraction process in this case is a classifier that decides whether a new observation at that pixel comes form the learned background distribution. Assuming the foreground distribution is uniform, this amounts to putting a threshold on the tail of the Gaussian likelihood, i.e., the classification rule reduces to marking a pixel as foreground if

$$\|x_t - \hat{\mu}\| > \text{threshold},$$

where the threshold is typically set to $k\hat{\sigma}$. Here $\hat{\mu}$ and $\hat{\sigma}$ are the estimated mean and standard deviation and k is a free parameter. The standard deviation σ even can be assumed to be the same for all pixels. So, literally, this simple model reduces to subtracting a background image B from the each new frame I_t and checking the difference against a threshold. In such cases, the background image B is the mean of the history background frames.

For the case of color images, as well as where the observation at the pixel is a high-dimensional vector, $x_t \in \mathbb{R}^d$, a multivariate Gaussian density can be used, i.e.,

$$P(x_t|\mathcal{B}) \approx \mathcal{N}(\mu, \Sigma) = \frac{1}{\sqrt{2\pi|\Sigma|}}e^{\frac{-1}{2}(x_t-\mu)^\top\Sigma^{-1}(x_t-\mu)},$$

where $\mu \in \mathbb{R}^d$ is the mean, and $\Sigma \in \mathbb{R}^{d\times d}$ is the covariance matrix of the distribution. Typically, the color channels are assumed to be independent. Therefore, the covariance is a diagonal matrix, which reduces a multivariate Gaussian to a product of single Gaussians, one for each color channel. More discussion about dealing with color will be presented in Section 2.8

This basic single Gaussian model can be made adaptive to slow changes in the scene (for example, gradual illumination changes) by recursively updating the mean with each new frame to maintain a background image

$$B_t = \frac{t-1}{t}B_{t-1} + \frac{1}{t}I_t,$$

where $t \geq 1$. Here, B_t denotes the background image computed up to frame t. Obviously, this update mechanism does not forget the history and, therefore, the effect of new images on the model tends to zero. This is not suitable when the goal is to adapt the model to illumination changes. Instead, the mean and variance can be computed over a sliding window of time. However, a more practical and efficient solution is to recursively update the model via temporal blending, also known as exponential forgetting, i.e.,

$$B_t = \alpha I_t + (1 - \alpha) B_{t-1}. \tag{2.2}$$

The parameter α controls the speed of forgetting old background information. This update equation is a low-pass filter with a gain factor α that effectively separates the slow temporal process (background) from the fast process (moving objects). Notice that the computed background image is no longer the sample mean over the history but captures the central tendency over a window in time [Gao and Boult, 2000].

This basic adaptive model seems to be a direct extension to earlier work on change detection between two images. One of the earliest papers that suggested this model, with a full justification of the background and foreground distributions, is the paper by Donohoe et al. [1988]. Karmann and von Brandt [1990] and Karmann et al. [1990] used a similar recursive update model without explicit assumption about the background process. Koller et al. [1994] used a similar model for traffic monitoring. A similar model was also used in early people-tracking systems, such as the Pfinder [Wern et al., 1997].

2.4.2 A MIXTURE GAUSSIAN BACKGROUND MODEL

The single-Gaussian background model is quite limited, since it assumes the intensity at any pixel is constant and the only source of variation is additive Gaussian noise. Typically, in outdoor environments, with moving trees and bushes, the scene background is not completely static. For example, one pixel can be the image of the sky in one frame, a tree leaf in another frame, a tree branch in a third frame, and some mixture subsequently. In each of these situations the pixel will have a different intensity (color). Therefore, a single Gaussian assumption for the probability density function of the pixel intensity will not hold. Instead, a generalization based on a Mixture of Gaussians (MoG) has been proposed in Friedman and Russell [1997], Rowe and Blake [1996], Stauffer and Grimson [1998, 1999] to model such variations. This model was introduced by Friedman and Russell [1997], where a mixture of three Gaussian distributions was used to model the pixel value for traffic-surveillance applications. The pixel intensity was modeled as a weighted mixture of three Gaussian distributions corresponding to road, shadow, and vehicle distribution. Fitting a mixture of Gaussian (MoG) model can be achieved using the Expectation Maximization (EM) algorithm [Dempster et al., 1977]. However this is impractical for a real-time background-subtraction application. An incremental EM algorithm [Neal and Hinton, 1993] was used to learn and update the parameters of the model.

Stauffer and Grimson [1998, 1999] proposed a generalization to the previous approach. The intensity of a pixel is modeled by a mixture of K Gaussian distributions (K is a small number from 3–5). The mixture is weighted by the frequency with which each of the Gaussians explains the background. The likelihood that a certain pixel has intensity x_t at time t is estimated as

$$p(x_t | \mathcal{B}) = \sum_{i=1}^{K} w_{i,t} G(x_t; \mu_{i,t}, \Sigma_{i,t}), \tag{2.3}$$

where $G(\cdot; \mu_{i,t}, \Sigma_{i,t})$ is a Gaussian density function with a mean $\mu_{i,t}$ and covariance

$$\Sigma_{i,t} = \sigma_{i,t}^2 \mathbf{I}.$$

Here, $w_{i,t}$ is the weight for the i-th Gaussian components. The subscript t indicates that the weight, the mean, and the covariance of each component are updated at each time step.

The parameters of the distributions are updated recursively using online approximations of the EM algorithm. The mixture is weighted by the frequency with which each of the Gaussians explains the background, i.e., a new pixel value is checked against the existing K Gaussians, and, when a match is found, the weight for that distribution is updated as follows

$$w_{i,t} = (1 - \alpha) w_{i,t-1} + \alpha M(i, t),$$

where $M(i, t)$ is an indicator variable which is 1 if the i-th component is matched, 0 otherwise. The parameter of the matched distributions are updated as follows

$$\mu_t = (1 - \rho) \mu_{t-1} + \rho x_t,$$

$$\sigma_t^2 = (1 - \rho) \sigma_{t-1}^2 + \rho (x_t - \mu_t)^T (x_t - \mu_t).$$

The parameters α and ρ are two learning rates for the algorithm. The K distributions are ordered based on w_j / σ_j^2 and the first B distributions are used as a model of the background of the scene where B is estimated as

$$B = \arg\min_b \left(\sum_{j=1}^{b} w_j > T \right). \tag{2.4}$$

The threshold T is the fraction of the total weight given to the background model. Background subtraction is performed by marking any pixel that is more that 2.5 standard deviations away from any of the B distributions as a foreground pixel.

The MoG background model was shown to perform very well in indoor situations and also in outdoor situations with limited variations. It is the most widely used approach for background subtraction because of its simplicity and efficiency. Many variations have been suggested to the Stauffer and Grimson's model [Stauffer and Grimson, 1999], e.g., [Harville, 2002, Javed et al.,

2002, Mittal and Huttenlocher, 2000], etc. The model also was used with different feature spaces and/or with a subspace representation. Gao and Boult [2000] studied the statistical error characteristic of MoG background models. For a comprehensive survey on the variations suggested on the MoG model, we refer the readers to Bouwmans et al. survey [Bouwmans et al., 2008].

2.5   NON-PARAMETRIC BACKGROUND MODELS

In outdoor scenes, typically there are a wide range of variations, which can be very fast. Outdoor scenes usually contain dynamic areas, such as waving trees and bushes, rippling water, or ocean waves. Such fast variations are part of the scene background. Figure 2.3 shows an example of such fast variations. Modeling such dynamic areas requires a more flexible representation of the background probability distribution at each pixel. This motivates the use of a non-parametric density estimator for background modeling [Elgammal et al., 2000]. The intuition is to be able to deal with any multimodal background distribution without any assumption about the model.

2.5.1   KERNEL DENSITY ESTIMATION (KDE)

A particular non-parametric technique that estimates the underlying density and is quite general is the kernel density estimation (KDE) technique [Duda et al., 2000, Scott, 1992]. Given a sample $S = \{x_i\}_{i=1..N}$ from a distribution with density function $p(x)$, an estimate $\hat{p}(x)$ of the density at x can be calculated using

$$\hat{p}(x) = \frac{1}{N} \sum_{i=1}^{N} K_\sigma(x - x_i), \tag{2.5}$$

where K_σ is a kernel function (sometimes called a "window" function) with a bandwidth (scale) σ such that $K_\sigma(t) = \frac{1}{\sigma} K(\frac{t}{\sigma})$. The kernel function K should satisfy $K(t) \geq 0$ and $\int K(t)dt = 1$. We can think of equation 2.5 as estimating the probability density function by averaging the effect of a set of local functions centered at each data point. Alternatively, since the kernel function is symmetric, we can also regard this computation as averaging the effect of a kernel function centered at the estimation point and evaluated at each data point. That is, a kernel estimator computes a weighted local average of the data points in a window around the estimation point.

A variety of kernel functions with different properties have been used in the literature of non-parametric estimation. Typically, kernel functions are symmetric and unimodal functions that fall off to zero rapidly away from the center, i.e., the kernel function should have finite local support and points beyond a certain window will have no contribution. The Gaussian function is typically used as a kernel for its continuity, differentiability, and locality properties, although it violates the finite support criterion [Elgammal, 2002]. Note that choosing the Gaussian as a kernel function is different from fitting the distribution to a mixture of Gaussian model. Here, the Gaussian is only used as a function to weight the data points. Unlike parametric fitting of a mixture of Gaussians, kernel density estimation is a more general approach that does not assume any specific shape for the density function, and does not require model parameter estimation.

Table 2.1: Example of kernel functions

Kernel	Equation
Uniform	$U(-1,1)$
Triangle	$(1-\mid t \mid)$
Epanechnikov	$\frac{3}{4}(1-t^2)$
Biweight	$\frac{15}{16}(1-t^2)^2$
Gaussian	$N(0,1)$
Cosine arch	$\frac{\pi}{4}cos\frac{\pi}{2}t$
Double Exponential	$\frac{1}{2}e^{-|t|}$
Double Epanechnikov	$3\mid t\mid(1-\mid t\mid)$

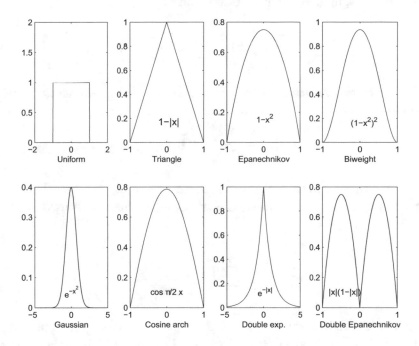

Figure 2.4: Example of kernel functions typically used in KDE.

Kernel density estimators asymptotically converge to any density function with sufficient samples [Duda et al., 2000, Scott, 1992]. In fact, all other non-parametric density estimation methods, e.g., histograms, can be shown to be asymptotically kernel methods [Scott, 1992]. This property makes these techniques quite general and applicable to many vision problems where the underlying density is not known [Comaniciu, 2000, Elgammal, 2002]. We can avoid having to store the complete data set by weighting a subset of the samples as

$$\hat{p}(x) = \sum_{x_i \in B} \alpha_i K_\sigma (x - x_i),$$

where α_i are weighting coefficients that sum up to one and B is a sample subset. A good discussion of KDE techniques can be found in Scott [1992] and Elgammal [2002].

2.5.2   KDE BACKGROUND MODELS

Elgammal et al. [2000] introduced a background-modeling approach based on kernel density estimation. Let $x_1, x_2, ..., x_N$ be a sample of intensity values for a pixel. Here the sample directly constitutes the background model ($\mathcal{B}$). Given this sample, we can obtain an estimate of the probability density function of a pixel's intensity value (i.e., compute the likelihood given the background model) using kernel density estimation as

$$p(x_t|\mathcal{B})\frac{1}{N} \sum_{i=1}^{N} K_\sigma (x - x_i). \tag{2.6}$$

This estimate can be generalized to use color features or other high-dimensional features by using kernel products as

$$p(x_t|\mathcal{B}) = \frac{1}{N} \sum_{i=1}^{N} \prod_{j=1}^{d} K_{\sigma_j} (x_t^j - x_i^j), \tag{2.7}$$

where x_t^j is the j-th dimension of the feature at time t and K_{σ_j} is a kernel function with bandwidth σ_j in the jth color space dimension. If the Gaussian function is used as a kernel, then the density can be estimated as

$$p(x_t|\mathcal{B}) = \frac{1}{N} \sum_{i=1}^{N} \prod_{j=1}^{d} \frac{1}{\sqrt{2\pi\sigma_j^2}} e^{-\frac{1}{2}\frac{(x_t^j - x_i^j)^2}{\sigma_j^2}}. \tag{2.8}$$

Using this probability estimate, the pixel is considered a foreground pixel if $p(x_t|\mathcal{B}) < th$, where the threshold th is a global threshold over all the image, which can be adjusted to achieve a desired percentage of false positives. The estimate in Eq. 2.7 is based on the most recent N samples used in the computation. Therefore, adaptation of the model can be achieved simply by adding new samples and ignoring older samples [Elgammal et al., 2000], i.e., using a sliding window over time. Figure 2.5-b shows the estimated background probability where brighter pixels represent lower background probability pixels.

Practically, the probability estimation in Eq. 2.8 can be calculated in a very fast way using pre-calculated lookup tables for the kernel function values given the intensity value difference,

(a)   (b)

Figure 2.5: Example of probability estimation using a non-parametric model (a) original image. (b) Estimated probability image. From Elgammal et al. [2000] "Non-Parameteric Model for Background Subtraction" (Springer ©2000).

$(x_t - x_i)$, and the kernel function bandwidth. Moreover, a partial evaluation of the sum in equation 2.8 is usually sufficient to surpass the threshold at most image pixels, since most of the image is typically from the background. This allows a real-time implementation of the approach.

This non-parametric technique for background subtraction was introduced in Elgammal et al. [2000] and has been tested for a wide variety of challenging background subtraction problems in a variety of setups and was found to be robust and adaptive. We refer the reader to Elgammal et al. [2000] for details about the approach; such as model adaptation and false detection suppression. Figures 2.6 shows two detection results for targets in a wooded area where tree branches move heavily and the target is highly occluded. Figure 2.7-top shows the detection results using an omni-directional camera. The targets are camouflaged and walking through the woods. Figure 2.7-bottom shows the detection result for a rainy day where the background model adapts to account for different rain and lighting conditions.

One major issue that needs to be addressed when using a kernel density estimation technique is the choice of suitable kernel bandwidth (scale). Theoretically, as the number of samples increases the bandwidth should decrease. Practically, since only a finite number of samples are used, and the computation must be performed in real time, the choice of suitable bandwidth is essential. Too small bandwidth will lead to a ragged density estimate, while a too wide bandwidth will lead to an over-smoothed density estimate [Duda et al., 2000, Elgammal, 2002]. Since the expected variations in pixel intensity over time are different from one location to another in the image, a different kernel bandwidth is used for each pixel. Also, a different kernel bandwidth is used for each color channel.

In Elgammal et al. [2000], a procedure was proposed for estimating the kernel bandwidth for each pixel as a function of the median of absolute differences between consecutive frames. To estimate the kernel bandwidth σ_j^2 for the jth color channel for a given pixel, the median absolute deviation for consecutive intensity values of the pixel is computed over the sample. That is, the median, m, of $| x_i - x_{i+1} |$ for each consecutive pair (x_i, x_{i+1}) in the sample is calculated independently for each color channel. The motivation behind the use of median of absolute deviation is that pixel intensities over time are expected to have jumps because different objects (e.g., sky, branch, leaf, and mixtures when an edge passes through the pixel) are projected onto the same pixel at different times. Since we are measuring deviations between two consecutive intensity values, the pair (x_i, x_{i+1}) usually comes from the same local-in-time distribution, and only a few pairs are expected to come from cross distributions (intensity jumps). The median is a robust estimate and should not be affected by few jumps. If this local-in-time distribution is assumed to be a Gaussian $N(\mu, \sigma^2)$, then the distribution for the deviation $(x_i - x_{i+1})$ is also Gaussian $N(0, 2\sigma^2)$. Since this distribution is symmetric, the median of the absolute deviations, m, is equivalent to the quarter percentile of the deviation distribution. That is,

$$Pr(N(0, 2\sigma^2) > m) = 0.25 ,$$

and therefore the standard deviation of the first distribution can be estimated as

$$\sigma = \frac{m}{0.68\sqrt{2}} .$$

Since the deviations are integer gray scale (color) values, linear interpolation can be used to obtain more accurate median values. In Mittal and Paragios [2004], an adaptive approach for estimation of kernel bandwidth was proposed. Parag et al. [2006] proposed an approach using boosting to evaluate different kernel bandwidth choices for bandwidth selection.

2.5.3   KDE-BACKGROUND PRACTICE AND OTHER NON-PARAMETRIC MODELS

One of the drawbacks of the KDE background model is the requirement to store a large number of history samples for each pixel. In KDE literature, many approaches were proposed to avoid storing a large number of samples. Within the context of background modeling, Piccardi and Jan [2004] proposed an efficient mean-shift approach to estimate the modes of a pixel's history PDF, then a few number of Gaussians were used to model the PDF. Mean shift is a non-parametric iterative mode-seeking procedure [Cheng, 1995, Comaniciu and Meer, 1999, Fukunaga and Hostetler, 1975]. With the same goal of reducing memory requirement, Han et al. [2004] proposed a sequential kernel density estimation approach where variable bandwidth mean shift was used to detect the density modes. Unlike mixture of Gaussian methods, where the number of Gaussians is fixed, technique such as Piccardi and Jan [2004] and Han et al. [2004] can adaptively estimate a variable number of modes to represent the density, therefore keeping the flexibility of a non-parametric model, while achieving the efficiency of a parametric model.

Efficient implementation of KDE can be achieved through building look-up tables for the kernel values as functions of the deviations, which facilitates real-time performance. The Fast Gauss Transform has been proposed for efficient computation of KDE Elgammal et al. [2001]. However, the Fast Gauss Transform is only justifiable when the number of samples required for density estimation is large, as well as when there is a need for estimation at many pixels in batches. For example, Fast Gauss implementation was effectively used in a layered background representation [Patwardhan et al., 2008].

Many variations have been suggested to the basic non-parametric KDE background model. In practice, non-parametric KDE has been used at the pixel level, as well as at the region level, and in a domain-range representation to model a scene background. For example, in Patwardhan et al. [2008], a layered representation was used to model the scene background where the distribution of each layer is modeled using KDE. Such layered representation facilitates detecting the foreground under static or dynamic background and in the presence of nominal camera motion. In Sheikh and Shah [2005], KDE was used in a joint domain-range representation of image pixel (R, G, B, x, y), which exploits the spatial correlation between neighboring pixels. Parag et al. [2006] proposed an approach for feature selection for the KDE framework, where boosting-based ensemble learning was used to combine different features. The approach also can be used to evaluate different kernels bandwidth choices for bandwidth selection. Recently, Sheikh et al. [2009] used a KDE approach in a joint domain-range representation within a foreground/background segmentation framework from a freely moving camera, as will be discussed in Chapter 3.

2.6   OTHER BACKGROUND MODELS

The statistical models for background subtraction that are described in this section are the basis for many other algorithms in the literature. There is a vast literature on background subtraction, which cannot be covered comprehensively in this chapter. In this section we briefly describe some of the other background models available and highlight their features.

2.6.1   PREDICTIVE-FILTERING BACKGROUND MODELS

In Toyama et al. [1999], linear prediction using the Wiener filter is used to predict pixel intensity, given a recent history of values. The prediction coefficients are recomputed, each frame from the sample covariance to achieve adaptivity. Linear prediction using the Kalman Filter was also used in Karmann and von Brandt [1990], Karmann et al. [1990], Koller et al. [1994], such models assume a single Gaussian distribution of the pixel process. In Soatto et al. [2001], an Auto Regressive Moving Average Model (ARMA) model was proposed for modeling dynamic textures. ARMA is a first-order linear prediction model. In Zhong and Sclaroff [2003], an ARMA model was used for background modeling of scenes with dynamic texture where a robust Kalman filter was used to update the model [Kalman, 1960].

Figure 2.6: Example background-subtraction detection results: Left: original frames, Right: detection results.

2.6.2 HIDDEN MARKOV MODEL BACKGROUND SUBTRACTION

Another approach to model a wide range of variations in the pixel intensity is to represent these variations as discrete states corresponding to modes of the environment, e.g., lights on/off, cloudy/sunny. Hidden Markov Models (HMM) have been used for this purpose in Rittscher et al. [2000] and Stenger et al. [2001]. In Rittscher et al. [2000], a three-state HMM has been used to model the intensity of a pixel for traffic monitoring applications where the three states correspond to the background, shadow, and foreground. The use of HMMs imposes a temporal continuity constraint on the pixel intensity, i.e., if the pixel is detected as a part of the foreground, then it is expected to remain part of the foreground for a period of time before switching back to be part of the background. In Stenger et al. [2001], the topology of the HMM representing global image intensity is learned while learning the background. At each global intensity state, the pixel intensity is modeled using a single Gaussian. It was shown that the model is able to learn simple scenarios like switching the lights on-off.

Figure 2.7: Top: Detection of camouflaged targets from an omni-directional camera. Bottom: Detection result for a rainy day.

2.6.3 SUBSPACE METHODS FOR BACKGROUND SUBTRACTION

Subspace background-subtraction models learn a subspace that spans a sample history image from the scene background. A new frame is then projected to that subspace, the vector between input image and its subspace projection is used to detect outlier pixels (foreground) by comparing against a threshold. Oliver et al. [2000] used Principle Component Analysis (PCA) to learn the subspace, denoted by eigen-background. Unlike the aforementioned approaches, which are mainly pixel-based, subspace methods typically deal with the whole image as a sample in a high-dimensional space. This has the advantage of capturing the spatial correlation between pixels. However, the disadvantage is that large foreground regions can easily throw out the estimation process, since the subspace projection and reconstruction is a least-squares approximation, that is sensitive to outliers. Robust PCA has been used to enhance the performance of the method. Incremental versions of PCA were also proposed to maintain the background [Li, 2004, Rymel et al., 2004, Skocaj and Leonardis, 2003, Wang et al., 2007]. Other subspace methods have been used instead of PCA, including Independent Component Analysis (ICA) [Tsai and Lai, 2009, Yamazaki et al., 2006] and Nonnegative Matrix Factorization (NMF) [Bucak and Gunsel, 2009].

2.6.4   NEURAL NETWORK MODELS

In Maddalena and Petrosino [2008], a biologically inspired non-parametric background-subtraction approach was proposed where a self-organizing artificial neural network model was used to model the pixel process. Each pixel is modeled with a sample arranged in a shared 2D grid of nodes, where each node is represented with a weight vector with the same dimensionality as the input observation. An incoming pixel observation is mapped to the node whose weights are "most similar" to the input where a threshold function is used to decide background/foreground. The weights of each node are updated at each new frame, using a recursive filter similar to Eq. 2.2. An interesting feature of this approach is that the shared 2D grid of nodes allows the spatial relationships between pixels to be taken into account at both the detection and update phases.

2.7   FEATURES FOR BACKGROUND MODELING

Intensity has been the most commonly used feature for modeling the background. Alternatively, edge features have also been used to model the background. The use of edge features to model the background is motivated by the desire to have a representation of the scene background that is invariant to illumination changes, as will be discussed in Section 2.8. In Yang and Levine [1992], foreground edges are detected by comparing the edges in each new frame with an edge map of the background, which is called the background "primal sketch." The major drawback of using edge features to model the background is that it would only be possible to detect edges of foreground objects instead of the dense connected regions that result from pixel-intensity-based approaches. Fusion of intensity and edge information was used in Huerta et al. [2009], Jabri et al. [2000], Mckenna et al. [2000], Zhang et al. [2006]. Among many other feature studied, optical flow was used in Mittal and Paragios [2004] to help capture background dynamics. A general framework for feature selection based on boosting for background modeling was proposed in Parag et al. [2006].

Besides pixel-based approaches, block-based approaches have also been used for modeling the background. Block matching has been extensively used for change detection between consecutive frames. In Hsu et al. [1984], each image block is fit to a second-order bivariate polynomial and the remaining variations are assumed to be noise. A statistical likelihood test is then used to detect blocks with significant change. In Matsuyama et al. [2000], each block was represented with its median template over the background learning period and its block standard deviation. Subsequently, at each new frame, each block is correlated with its corresponding template, and blocks with too much deviation relative to the measured standard deviation are considered to be foreground. The major drawback with block-based approaches is that the detection unit is a whole-image block and therefore they are only suitable for coarse detection.

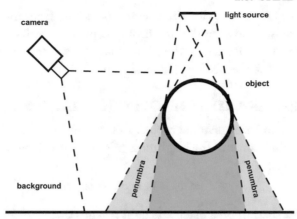

Figure 2.8: Illustration of cast shadow on the background: Cast shadows have a dark part (umbra) where a light source is totally occluded, and a soft transitional part (penumbra), where light is partially occluded [Stauder et al., 1999] (courtesy of Jürgen Stauder. IEEE ©1999).

2.8   SHADOW SUPPRESSION

Without carefully selecting the color space used in modeling the background, a background-subtraction process is bound to detect shadows of moving objects along with the objects themselves. While shadows of static objects can typically be learned as part of the background model, shadows cast by moving objects, i.e., dynamic shadows, constitute a severe challenge for foreground segmentation. Since the goal of background subtraction is to obtain accurate segmentation of moving foreground regions for further processing, it is highly desirable to detect such foreground regions without their cast shadows attached to them. This is particularly important for human motion analysis applications, since shadows attached to detected silhouettes would cause problems in fitting body limbs and estimating body posture (consider the example shown in Figure 2.9). Therefore, extensive research has addressed the detection/suppression of moving (dynamic) shadows. Avoiding the detection of shadows or suppressing the detected shadows can be achieved in color sequences by understanding how shadows affect color images. This is also useful to achieve a background model that is invariant to illumination changes.

Cast shadows have a dark part (umbra) where a light source is totally occluded, and a soft transitional part (penumbra) where light is partially occluded [Stauder et al., 1999] (see Figure 2.8). In visual surveillance scenarios, the penumbra shadows are common, since diffused and indirect light is common in indoor and outdoor scenes. Penumbra shadows can be characterized by a low value of intensity while preserving the chromaticity of the background, i.e., achromatic shadows. Therefore, most research on detecting shadows has focused on achromatic shadows [Cucchiara et al., 2003, Elgammal et al., 2000, Horprasert et al., 1999, e.g.]. In outdoor sittings the achromatic assumption is a simplification, since the diffused sky illumination causes the penumbra shadowed regions to differ in their chromaticity from their background. Recently, some researchers have also paid attention to chromatic penumbra shadows, as well as the detection of umbra-shadowed regions where their chromaticity is different from the chromaticity of the global illumination in the scene, e.g., [Huerta et al., 2009].

2.8.1   COLOR SPACES AND ACHROMATIC SHADOWS

Here, we describe an achromatic shadow model. Let us consider the RGB color space, which is a typical output of a color camera. The brightness of a pixel is a linear combination or the RGB channels, here denoted by I

$$I = w_r R + w_g G + w_b B.$$

When an object casts a shadow on a pixel, less light reaches that pixel and the pixel seems darker. Therefore, a shadow cast on a pixel can be characterized by a change of the brightness of that pixel such that

$$\tilde{I} = \alpha I,$$

where $\tilde{I}$ is the pixel's new brightness. A similar effect happens under certain changes in illumination, e.g., turning on/off the lights. Here $\alpha < 1$ for the case of shadow, which means the pixel is darker under shadow, while $\alpha > 1$ for the case of highlights, the pixel seems brighter. A change in the brightness of a pixel will affect all three color channels R, G, and B. Therefore, any background model based on the RGB space, and of course gray-scale imagery, is bound to detect moving shadows as foreground regions.

So, which color spaces are invariant or less sensitive to shadows and highlights? For simplicity, let us assume that the effect of the change in a pixel brightness is the same in the three channels. Therefore, the observed colors are αR, αG, αB. Any chromaticity measure of a pixel where the effect of the α factor is canceled, is in fact invariant to shadows and highlights. For example, Elgammal et al. [2000] proposed using chromaticity coordinates based on normalized RGB for modeling the background. Given three color variables, R, G and B, the chromaticity coordinates are defined as [Levine, 1985]

$$r = \frac{R}{R + G + B}, g = \frac{G}{R + G + B}, b = \frac{B}{R + G + B}. \tag{2.9}$$

Obviously, only two coordinates are enough to represent the chromaticity, since $r + g + b = 1$. The above equation describes a central projection to the plane $R + G + B = 1$. This is analogous to the transformation used to obtain CIE-xy chromaticity space from CIE-XYZ color space. The CIE-XYZ color space is related by a linear transformation to the RGB space [Burger and Burge, 2008]. The chromaticity space defined by the variable r, g is therefore analogous to the CIE-xy chromaticity space. It can be easily seen that the chromaticity variables r, g, b are invariant to achromatic shadows and highlights (according to our assumption), since the α factor does not have an effect on them. Figure 2.9 shows the results of detection using both (R, G, B) space and (r, g) space. The figure shows that using the chromaticity coordinates allows detection of the target without detecting its shadow.

Some other color spaces also have chromaticity variables that are invariant to achromatic shadows and highlights in the same way. For example, the Hue and Saturation variables in the HSV color space are invariant to the α factor, and, thus, insensitive to shadows and highlights, while the Value variable, which represents the brightness, is variant to them. Therefore, the HSV color space has been used in some background-subtraction algorithms that suppress shadows [e.g., Cucchiara et al., 2003]. Similarly, HSL and CIE-xy and CIE-$L^*a^*b^*$ spaces have the same property. On the other hand, the chromaticity variables in color spaces such as YUV, YIQ, YCbCr are not invariant to shadows and highlights, since they are just linear transformations from the RGB space.

Although using chromaticity coordinates helps in the suppression of shadows, they have the disadvantage of losing lightness information. Lightness is related to the differences in whiteness, blackness, and grayness between different objects [Hall, 1979]. For example, consider the case where the target wears a white shirt and walks against a gray background. In this case there is no color information. Since both white and gray have the same chromaticity coordinates, the target will not be detected using only chromaticity variables. In fact, in the r, g space, as well as the CIE-xy space, all the gray lines (R=G=B) project to the point (1/3, 1/3) in the space. Therefore, there is no escape from using a brightness variable. Almost all color-based background-subtraction models use three-channel color spaces that include brightness information. However, there is a great advantage in separating the shadow-variant brightness variable from the shadow-invariant chromaticity variables. Elgammal et al. [2000] proposed using a third "lightness" variable $s = R + G + B$, besides r, g. While the chromaticity variable r, g is not expected to change under shadow, s is expected to change within limits, which corresponds to the expected shadows and highlights in the scene. Similarly, the use of CIE-xy besides the variable Y from CIE-XYZ, or the use of HSV, HLS, and CIE-$L^*a^*b^*$ offers the same desired separation.

2.8.2   ALGORITHMIC APPROACHES FOR SHADOW DETECTION

The above discussion highlights a way to discriminate between foreground regions and cast shadows. A foreground pixel is expected to show chromaticity distortion or a large brightness distortion, while a cast shadow pixel is expected to show darker brightness than its corresponding background model. Most approaches for shadow suppression rely on this reasoning of separating the chromaticity distortion from brightness distortion, where each of these distortions are treated differently [e.g., Cucchiara et al., 2003, Elgammal et al., 2000, Horprasert et al., 1999, Huerta et al., 2009, Kim et al., 2004]. However, the definition of what is the chromaticity distortion and what is the brightness distortion differs. Approaches that use a color space that separates the shadow-invariant chromaticity variables from the shadow-variant brightness variable can directly define chromaticity distortion in the chromaticity space and brightness distortion in the brightness space [Cucchiara et al., 2003, Elgammal et al., 2000, e.g]. In contrast, approaches that

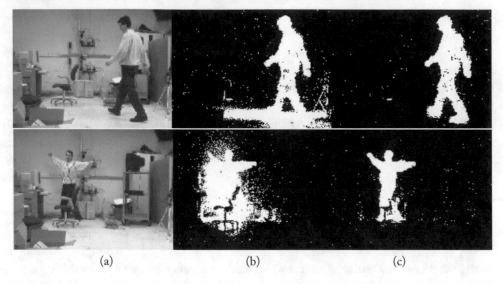

(a)   (b)   (c)

Figure 2.9: (a) Original frames, (b) Detection using (R, G, B) color space, (c) detection using chromaticity coordinates (r, g) and the lightness variable s. From Elgammal et al. [2000] "Non-Parameteric Model for Background Subtraction" (Springer ©2000).

directly use RGB have to define chromaticity and brightness distortion models [Horprasert et al., 1999, Huerta et al., 2009, e.g.].

Horprasert et al. [1999, 2000] defined the brightness and color distortions using a chromatic cylinder model. Each pixel in the background is represented by its chromaticity line in the RGB space. For pixel i, this is the line connecting the expected RGB value of the pixel, E_i, to the origin. An illustration can be seen in Figure 2.10. Here a single Gaussian background model is assumed. The RGB color of an observed pixel, I_i is projected to that pixel's chromaticity line. The color distortion, CD_i is defined as the orthogonal distance between the observation and its expected chromaticity line, i.e.,

$$CD_i = \|I_i - \alpha_i E_i\|.$$

The projection of the observation to the chromaticity line defines the brightness distortion α_i. These two measurements were used to classify an observation to either background, foreground, shadows, or highlights. The rationale is that the brightness distortion would be less than one if the pixel is darker than its expected value (shadow), while it would be greater than one if the pixel is brighter (highlights). The pixel is consider a moving foreground if it exhibits a color distortion or brightness distortion above certain thresholds (for details, see Horprasert et al. [1999, 2000]). Effectively, this assumes that the appearance of a background pixel varies around the expected value within a cylinder whose axis is the chromaticity line. Figure 2.12 shows examples of using that model.

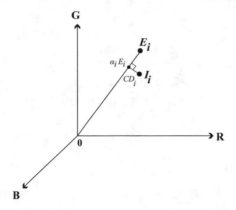

Figure 2.10: An illustration of the chromaticity distortion and brightness distortion model of Horprasert et al. [Horprasert et al., 1999, 2000]. I_i is the observed color of pixel i. E_i is the expected background value for that pixel. The projection of I_i into OE_i defines the brightness distortion α_i and color distortion CD_i. Courtesy of Thanarat H. Chalidabhongse.

Notice that the orthogonal distance between an observed pixel's RGB color and a chromaticity line is affected by the brightness of that pixel. In contrast, measuring the angle between the expected chromaticity line and the observation gives an estimate of the chromaticity distortion independent of the brightness. Measuring the angular distortion implies a chromaticity cone model around the expected chromaticity line, a mode that was proposed by Huerta et al. [2009] (see Figure 2.11). Notice that the angular distortion is directly proportional to measuring distances in the $r - g$ space or in the CIE-xy space, where points in these spaces are central projections of the chromaticity lines. A chromaticity cone will project into an ellipsoid in these spaces. Therefore, models that use these chromaticity spaces to model the background appearance [Elgammal et al., 2000, e.g.] implicitly assume a chromaticity cone distortion model.

Another class of algorithms for shadow suppression are approaches that depend on image gradient to model the scene background. The idea is that texture information in the background will be consistent under shadow, hence using the image gradient orientation as a feature will be invariant to cast shadows, except at the shadow boundary. These approaches utilize a background edge or gradient model besides the chromaticity model to detect shadows [e.g., Huerta et al., 2009, 2013, Jabri et al., 2000, Mckenna et al., 2000, Zhang et al., 2006]. Huerta et al. [2009] propose a multistage approach to detect chromatic shadows. In the first stage, potential shadow regions are detected by fusing color (using the invariant chromaticity cone model described above) and gradient information. In the second stage, pixels in these regions are classified using different cues, including spatial and temporal analysis of chrominance, brightness, and texture distortion. A measure of diffused sky lighting was also used in the analysis, denoted by "bluish effect."

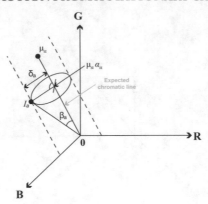

Figure 2.11: Illustration of a conic chromatic distortion model [Huerta et al., 2009] (courtesy of Ivan Huerta. IEEE ©2009).

Figure 2.13 illustrates the flow of the approach. The approach can successfully detect chromatic shadows (for more details, see Huerta et al. [2009, 2013]).

2.9   TRADEOFFS IN BACKGROUND MAINTENANCE

As discussed in Section 2.1, there are different changes that can occur in a scene background, which can be classified to: Illumination changes, Motion Changes, Structural Changes. The goal of background maintenance is to be able to cope with these changes and keep an updated version of the scene background model. In parametric background models, recursive update in the form of Eq. 2.2 (or some variant of it) is typically used for background maintenance [e.g., Karmann and von Brandt, 1990, Koller et al., 1994, Stauffer and Grimson, 1999]. In non-parametric models, the sample of each pixel history is updated continuously to achieve adaptability [Elgammal et al., 2000, Mittal and Paragios, 2004]. These recursive updates, along with careful choice of the color space, are typically enough to deal with both the illumination changes and motion changes previously described.

The most challenging case is where changes are introduced to the background (objects moved in or from the background) denoted here by "Structural Changes." For example, if a vehicle came and parked in the scene. A background process should detect such a car but should also adapt it to the background model in order to be able to detect other targets that might pass in front of it. Similarly, if a vehicle that was already part of the scene moved out, a false detection "hole" will appear in the scene where that vehicle was parked. There are many examples similar to these scenarios. Toyama et al. [1999] denoted these situations "sleeping person" and "walking person" scenarios.

Here we point out two interwound tradeoffs that associate with maintaining any background model.

Figure 2.12: An illustration showing the detection using the model of Horprasert et al. [Horprasert et al., 1999, 2000]. At the middle of the sequence, half of the fluorescence lamps are turned off. The result shows that the system still detects the moving object successfully (courtesy of Thanarat H. Chalidabhongse).

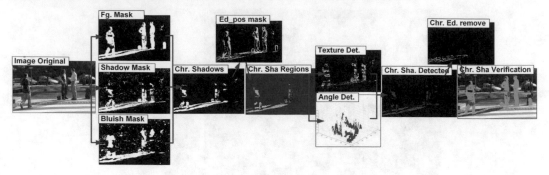

Figure 2.13: Illustration of the chromatic shadow detection approach of Huerta et al. [2009] (courtesy of Ivan Huerta. IEEE ©2009).

Background update rate: The speed or the frequency at which a background model gets updated highly influences the performance of the process. In most parametric models, the learning rate α in Eq. 2.2 controls the speed in which the model adapts to changes. In non-parametric models, the frequency in which new samples are added to the model has the same effect. Fast model update makes the model able to rapidly adapt to scene changes, such as fast illumination changes, which leads to high sensitivity in foreground/background classification. However, the model can also adapt to targets in the scene if the update is done blindly in all pixels or errors occur in masking out foreground regions. Slow update is safer to avoid integrating any transient changes to the model. However, the classifier will lose its sensitivity in case of fast scene changes.

Selective vs. blind update: Given a new pixel observation, there are two alternative mechanisms to update a background model: (1) Selective Update: update the model only if the pixel is classified as a background sample. (2) Blind Update: just update the model regardless of the classification outcome. Selective update is commonly used by masking out foreground-classified pixels from the update, since updating the model with foreground information would lead to increased false negative, e.g., holes in the detected targets. The problem with selective update is that any incorrect detection decision will result in persistent incorrect detection later, which is a deadlock situations as denoted by Karmann and von Brandt [1990]. For example, if a tree branch is displaced and stayed fixed in the new location for a long time, it would be continually detected. This is what leads to the "Sleeping/Walking person" problems as denoted in Toyama et al. [1999].

Blind update does not suffer from this deadlock situation since it does not involve any update decisions; it allows intensity values that do not belong to the background to be added to the model. This might lead to more false negatives as targets erroneously become part of the model. This effect can be reduced if the update rate is slow.

The interwound effects of these two tradeoffs is shown in Table 2.2. Most background models chose a selective update approach and try to avoid the effects of detection errors by using

Table 2.2: Tradeoffs in background maintenance

	Fast Update	Slow Update
Selective Update	Highest sensitivity Adapts to fast illumination changes Bound to Deadlocks	Less sensitivity Bound to Deadlocks
Blind Update	Adapts to targets (more False Negatives) No deadlocks	Slow adaptation No deadlocks

a slow update rate. However, this is bound to deadlocks. In Elgammal et al. [2000], the use of a combination of two models was proposed: a short-term model (selective and fast) and a long-term model (blind and slow). This combination tries to achieve high sensitivity and, at the same time, avoids deadlocks.

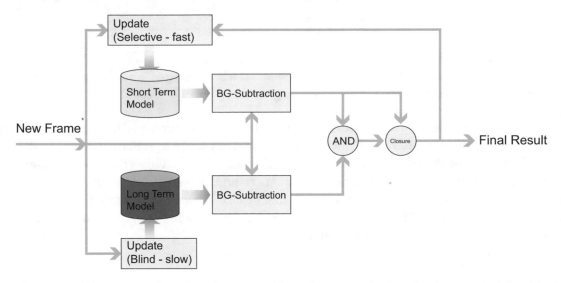

Figure 2.14: Illustration of using a short term (fast selective update) and a long term (slow blind update) background model for detection [Elgammal et al., 2000].

Several approaches have been proposed for dealing with specific scenarios with structural changes. The main problem is that dealing with such changes requires a higher level of reasoning about what are the objects causing such structural changes (vehicle, person, animal) and what should be done with them, which mostly depends on the application. Such a high level of reasoning is typically beyond the design goal of the background process, which is mainly a low-level process that knows only about pixels' appearance.

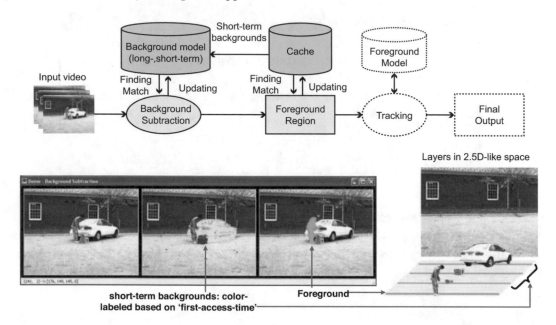

Figure 2.15: An overview of Kim et al. approach [Kim et al., 2005] with short-term background layers: the foreground and the short-term backgrounds can be interpreted in a different temporal order. Figure from Kim et al. [2005] (courtesy of Kyungnam Kim. Springer ©2005).

The idea of using multiple background models was further developed by Kim et al. [2005] to address scene structure changes in an elegant way. In that work, a layered background model was used where a long-term background model is used besides several multiple short-term background models that capture temporary changes in the background. An object that comes to the scene and stops is represented by a short-term background (layer). Therefore, if a second object passes in front of the stopped object, it will also be detected and represented as a layer as well. Figure 2.14 shows an overview of the approach and detection results.

CHAPTER 3

Background Subtraction from a Moving Camera

Most of today's videos are captured from moving platforms, such as camera phones and cameras mounted on ground vehicles, robots, ariel drones, or soldiers, etc. Traditional background-subtraction algorithms are not applicable for such videos captured from a non-stationary platforms. Despite that there are applicable solutions for detecting objects in videos, as explained in Section 1.3, these solutions are far from being effective. The goal of the research in the area of background subtraction from a moving camera is to develop algorithms that can be as effective as traditional background subtraction but also applicable to moving-camera videos.

In this chapter we review traditional and recent work in this area. We start in Section 3.1 by describing the difficulties in defining what is the background in the case of a mobile camera. There have been some extensions of background-subtraction algorithms to make them able to deal with mobile cameras, where camera motion is known or scene geometry is restricted, such as stationary-mounted pan-tilt-zoom cameras, or videos captured from high altitudes (e.g. drones). Such extensions utilize motion compensation to generalize background subtraction to such videos. We review these extension in Section 3.2. Unfortunately, there is yet no effective solution for the case of videos captured from a freely moving camera. In Section 3.3 we present a short review on motion-segmentation approaches. Motion segmentation is a fundamental building block to recent approaches for moving-camera background subtraction. We follow that by a short review on layered-motion segmentation approaches, in Section 3.4. In Section 3.5 we describe some recent algorithms for background subtraction for freely moving cameras, which are based on motion segmentation.

3.1 DIFFICULTIES IN THE MOVING-CAMERA CASE

As discussed in Section 1.2, the definition of what is foreground and what is background is ambiguous in the case of a video captured from a moving camera. A successful moving-camera background subtraction should utilize and integrate various perceptual cues to segment the foreground. The cues should include the following.

Motion discontinuity: Objects and image regions that are moving independently from the rest of the scene.

Depth discontinuity: Objects that are closer to the camera than the rest of the scene.

Appearance discontinuity: Salient objects or image regions that look different from the surrounding.

Familiar shape: Image regions that look like familiar shapes; i.e., object of interest such as people, vehicle, and animals.

None of these cues by itself is enough to solve the problem, and, therefore, integrating these four cues, besides high-level reasoning about the scene semantics, is necessary. The decision of foreground/background separation is not only low-level discontinuity detection, but also a high-level semantic decision. In what follows we justify our argument.

There is a large literature on motion segmentation, which exploits motion discontinuity, however, these approaches do not necessarily aim at modeling scene background and segmenting the foreground layers. Fundamentally 3D motion segmentation by itself is not enough to separate the foreground from the background in case both of them constitute a rigid or close to rigid motion, e.g., a car parked in the street will have the same 3D motion as the rest of the scene. Apparent 2D motion (optical flow) is also not enough to properly segment objects; for example an articulated object will exhibit different apparent motion at different parts.

Similarly, depth discontinuity by itself is not enough, since objects of interest can be at a distance from the camera without much depth difference from the background. There has been a lot of interest recently in saliency detection from images as a pre-step for object categorization. However, most of these works use static images and do not exploit rich video information. The performance of such low-level saliency detection is far from being reliable in detecting foreground objects accurately. Similarly, as we discussed earlier in Section 1.3, the state-of-the-art object detection is far from being able to segment foreground objects with the desired accuracy.

The above discussion highlights the need for integrated approaches the problem that combine low-level vision cues, namely: motion discontinuity, depth discontinuity, and appearance saliency with high-level object and scene accumulated and learned models.

3.2   MOTION-COMPENSATION-BASED BACKGROUND-SUBTRACTION TECHNIQUES

Motion-compensation-based approaches estimate the global motion (the geometric transformation) between consecutive frames, or between each frame and an *extended background map*. These methods typically use a homography or a 2D affine transform to compensate for the motion. The extended background map is a representation of the scene background, and any of the traditional methods, such as a Gaussian model or a Mixture of Gaussian, can be used to statistically model the pixel process in this representation. Once a transformation is recovered between each frame and the background map, objects can be detected. However, the success of these approaches depends on the accuracy of the motion estimation, which depends on how the assumed motion model is suitable to the actual scene. The accuracy of the motion estimation can deteriorate as a result of the existence of foreground objects (independent motion), which do not follow the motion model assumption. Robust estimation of the motion parameter is typically needed to tolerate these two problems. However, even with robust estimation, residual error exists, and approaches for dealing with these errors have to take place.

Many surveillance applications involve monitoring planer scenes, for example a parking lot or an arial view. The geometric transformation between images of a given plane, under the pinhole camera model, can be characterized by a homography, a transformation between two projective planes which preserves lines [Hartley and Zisserman, 2004]. Let P be a 3D point on a plane and let p_1 be its image in the first camera, and p_2 be its image in the second camera. Using homogenous coordinates, the geometric transformation between $p_1 = [x_1, \ y_1, \ 1]^T$ and $p_2 = [x_2, \ y_2, \ 1]^T$ can be written as

$$\lambda p_1 = \mathbf{H}_{21} p_2. \tag{3.1}$$

Here λ is scale variable and $\mathbf{H}_{21}$ is a nonsingular 3×3 transformation matrix mapping the coordinates of p_2 to p_1. Similarly $\mathbf{H}_{12} = \mathbf{H}_{21}^{-1}$ is a transformation matrix from p_1 to p_2. Such a transformation is called 2D homography. A general 2D homography matrix $\mathbf{H}$ is defined as

$$\mathbf{H} = \left[\begin{array}{ccc} h_{11} & h_{12} & h_{13} \\ h_{21} & h_{22} & h_{23} \\ h_{31} & h_{32} & h_{33} \end{array} \right].$$

However, because equation 3.1 is defined up to a scale, a homography between two images involves only eight parameters, i.e., any of the nine parameters in $\mathbf{H}$ can be set to 1. Therefore, a homography between two images can be estimated from four point matches by solving a system of linear equations for the eight unknowns parameters in $\mathbf{H}$. Linear least-squares can be used to estimate homographies from many matches. Typically RANSAC [Fischler and Bolles, 1981] and its variants, such as MLESAC [Torr and Zisserman, 2000] are used to achieve robust estimation using many matches. Estimating a homography between two images means that we can directly map the coordinate of one image to another, and hence an image mosaic can be established. Therefore, if the camera is overlooking a planer scene, an image mosaic of that scene can be established and every frame can be mapped to that mosaic via its computed homography.

If the camera motion is pure rotation, or pure zoom (with no translation), the geometric transformation between images can also be modeled by a homography, without the need for the planer scene assumption. In particular, this is very relevant for surveillance applications since pan-tilt-zoom (PTZ) cameras are typically used. Physically, panning and tilting of a PTZ camera are not pure rotations since the rotation of the camera head is not around the center of projection. Therefore, a small translation is typically involved in the camera motion and hence a parallax effect.

Some of the early papers that aimed at detecting foreground objects from PTZ cameras used motion compensation between consecutive frames and then image differencing, i.e., these approaches do not maintain a background model. For example, Murray and Basu [1994] computed the coordinate transformation between two images analytically as a function of the pan and tilt angles, assuming they are known, based on the geometric model proposed earlier by Kanatani [1987]. On that model the coordinates (x_t, y_t) of a given pixel at the current frame and its corresponding coordinates at the previous frame (x_{t-1}, y_{t-1}) are related by

$$x_{t-1} = f \frac{x_t + \alpha \sin\theta y_t + f\alpha \cos\theta}{-\alpha \cos\theta x_t + \gamma y_t + f}, \tag{3.2}$$

$$y_{t-1} = f \frac{-\alpha \sin\theta x_t + y_t - f\gamma}{-\alpha \cos\theta x_t + \gamma y_t + f},$$

where f is the focal lens, α and γ are respectively the pan and tilt rotation between the two frames, and θ is initial tilt (inclination) of the camera. Murray and Basu [1994] showed that this relation remains valid with a small displacement of the lens center from the center of rotation. To compensate for the error in coordinate estimation, resulting from the small translation, adaptive morphology is used, where the size of the morphology filter is derived as a function of the noise level. The assumption of knowing the pan and tilt angle is reasonable in active vision application and in online PTZ surveillance systems. Araki et al. [2000] used least-median-of-squares to estimate an affine motion model between consecutive frames, and, after compensating for the motion, image difference was use to detect the foreground of each frame and a background model.

There have been several approaches for building a background model from a panning camera based on building an image mosaic and the use of a traditional mixture of Gaussian background model [e.g., Mittal and Huttenlocher, 2000, Rowe and Blake, 1996]. Mittal and Huttenlocher [2000] used image registration to align each new image to a panoramic background image. The background image is the mean of the highest weighted Gaussian from a mixture of Gaussian model used at each pixel. The registered image is then used to update the background model. Image registration is achieved in two steps, based on tracked features: first, an affine transformation is estimated using robust least squares; and it is then used as an initial solution to estimate a projective transformation through nonlinear optimization. Figure 3.1 illustrates an example of this approach. The figure shows the mosaic built from a sequence of 150 frames from an arial video and detection results for two frames.

Hayman and olof Eklundh [2003] also built a mixture of Gaussian mosaic background model. However, they use MLESAC [Torr and Zisserman, 2000] to estimate the pan and tilt angle between a given image and the mosaic, assuming the calibration parameters are known. Alternatively, Wada and Matsuyama [1996] proposed to use a virtual sphere, denoted by "appearance sphere" to map images taken by a PTZ camera, assuming pure rotation. Practically, they proposed a representation of the scene background as a finite set of images on a virtual polyhedral appearance model. Jin et al. [2008] modeled the scene as a set of planer regions where each background pixel is assumed to belong to one of these regions. homographies were used to rectify each region to its corresponding planer representation in the model.

Several approaches have been proposed to deal with the residual errors resulting from the parallax effect due to the small translation involved in the pan and tilt motion, as well as other sources of errors, such as sub-pixel camera motion, etc. Basically, most of these approaches boil down to pooling a background representation from an "uncertainty" region around each target

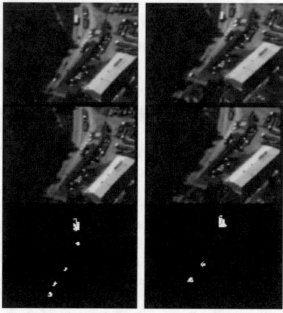

Figure 3.1: Example results from the approach of Mittal and Huttenlocher [Mittal and Huttenlocher, 2000]. Left: The background mosaic from an aerial video of 150 frames. Right top: Frame number 42 and 57; middle: synthesized frames with the moving objects removed; bottom: the corresponding moving objects detected. (Curtesy of Anurag Mittal. IEEE ©2000)

pixel in the background mosaic, with different statistical strategies. Ren et al. [2003] uses motion compensation to predict the position of each pixel in a background map, and model the uncertainty of that prediction by a spacial Gaussian distribution. This results in an uncertainty region for each pixel in the background map. A traditional single-Gaussian model is used at each pixel in the background map. Hayman and olof Eklundh [2003] showed that, given a Gaussian mixture component at each pixel in an uncertainty region, the mean and variance of the observation likelihood follows a so-called Mixel Distribution [Kitamoto, 2000], where its mean and variance can be computed efficiently by convolution with separable filters over the background mosaic.

3.3   MOTION SEGMENTATION

Motion segmentation refers to the problem of segmenting a video based on motion. It comes in different flavors depending on what is being segmented and what cues are used to achieve the segmentation. We can categorize motion segmentation algorithms into three classes.

Sparse Motion Segmentation: These are approaches that segment a set of extracted point trajectories using motion information alone. We refer to these as sparse motion-segmentation algorithms since they only use the motion information at sparse locations to segment them (not to be confused with algorithms that use sparsity).

Dense Motion Segmentation: These are algorithms that segment the entire set of pixels based on motion information, in addition to static cues, such as color or texture, to produce the segmentation.

Hybrid Motion-Segmentation Algorithms: These are hybrid algorithms that either use sparse motion-segmentation with static cues or dense motion segmentation using only motion.

Existing work in motion segmentation has largely assumed an affine camera model [Hartley and Zisserman, 2004, Mundy and Zisserman, 1992]. This assumption leads to the following formulation for the motion-segmentation problem [Costeira and Kanade, 1995].[1] Let us assume that there are N 3D points, denoted by $\{X_1, \cdots, X_N\}$ being tracked over F frames. This results in N point trajectories, where the trajectory for point X_j is denoted by $\{(x_i^j, y_i^j)|i = 1 \cdots F\}$. Here, (x_i^j, y_i^j) denotes the image coordinates of the i-th point in the jth frame. Let $\mathbf{X} = [X_1 X_2 \ldots X_N]$ be a $4 \times N$ matrix representing a set of N points in 3D using a homogeneous-coordinate system. According to the affine camera model, the relation between a 3D point X_i (in homogenous coordinate) and its projection in the j-th frame can be written as

$$\begin{bmatrix} x_i^j \\ y_i^j \end{bmatrix} = \mathbf{M}_j X_i,$$

where $\mathbf{M}_j$ is the 2×4 affine camera matrix[2] for the j-th frame. Let $\mathbf{M} = [\mathbf{M}_1 \ldots \mathbf{M}_F]^T$ be the $2F \times 4$ matrix formed by vertically concatenating F camera matrices, corresponding to F video frames. Such a model is only valid if the object on which the 3D points lie is rigid, where the motion of the object can be represented as motion of the camera with respect to a stationary object. Under the assumption of affine cameras, such camera matrices can be specified by the first two rows of the projection matrix. Taking the product of the two matrices $\mathbf{X}$ and $\mathbf{M}$, we get a matrix $\mathbf{W}$, where each column represents the projected locations of a single 3D point over F frames. The columns of $\mathbf{W}$ represent the trajectories in 2D image space, and can be written as

$$\mathbf{W} = \mathbf{MX}$$

$$\begin{bmatrix} x_1^1 & \cdots & x_1^N \\ y_1^1 & & y_1^N \\ \vdots & & \vdots \\ x_F^1 & & x_F^N \\ y_F^1 & & y_F^N \end{bmatrix} = \begin{bmatrix} \mathbf{M}_1 \\ \mathbf{M}_2 \\ \vdots \\ \mathbf{M}_F \end{bmatrix} [X_1 X_2 \ldots X_N].$$

---

[1]This factorization model was described in Costeira and Kanade [1995] for the orthographic camera, but it is also applicable to the case of affine cameras.

[2]If the translation is removed, the affine camera matrix can be written as 2×3 matrix.

Since the rank of a product of two matrices is bounded by the smallest dimension, the rank of the matrix of trajectories $\mathbf{W}$ is at most 4. It follows that trajectories generated from a single rigidly moving object lie on a subspace of dimension 4. Note that, in the factorization model of Tomasi and Kanade [1992], the translation is removed, which results in a $2F \times 3$ projection matrix $\mathbf{M}$. Therefore, the rank of the measurement matrix in that case is at most 3. The model described here is based on the more general model of Costeira and Kanade [1995], where the translation component is retained.

In general, when there are multiple moving objects, the columns of the trajectory matrix $\mathbf{W}$ will be sampled from multiple subspaces. Therefore, the motion segmentation problem can be formulated as that of subspace separation, i.e., assign each trajectory to one of the subspaces and estimate the subspaces.

In the literature, approaches to motion segmentation (and similarly subspace separation) can be roughly divided into four categories: factorization-based, statistical, algebraic, and spectral clustering.

Factorization-based Motion-Segmentation Approaches: Factorization-based methods, such as Ichimura [1999], Kanatani [2001], Tomasi and Kanade [1992], attempt to directly factorize a matrix of trajectories. These methods work well when the motions are independent. However, it is frequently the case that multiple rigid motions are dependent, such as in articulated motion. This has motivated the development of algorithms that handle dependent motion.

Statistical Motion-Segmentation Approaches: Statistical methods alternate between assigning points to subspaces and re-estimating the subspaces. For example, Gruber and Weiss [2004] used the Expectation-Maximization (EM) algorithm to tackle this clustering problem. Robust statistical methods, such as RANSAC [Fischler and Bolles, 1981], repeatedly fit an affine subspace to randomly sampled trajectories and measure the consensus with the remaining trajectories. The trajectories belonging to the subspace with the largest number of inliers are then removed and the procedure is repeated.

Algebraic Motion-Segmentation Approaches: Algebraic methods, such as GPCA [Vidal and Hartley, 2004] are generic subspace separation algorithms. They do not put assumptions on the relative orientation and dimensionality of motion subspaces. However, their complexity grows exponentially with the number of motions and the dimensionality of the ambient space.

Spectrial-clustering-based Motion-Segmentation Approaches: Spectral clustering-based methods [Brox and Malik, 2010, Ochs and Brox, 2012, Yan and Pollefeys, 2006, e.g.], use local information around the trajectories to compute a similarity matrix. They then use spectral clustering to cluster the trajectories into different subspaces. One such example is the approach by Yan and Pollefeys [2006], where neighbors around each trajectory are used to fit a subspace. An affinity matrix is then built by measuring the angles between subspaces. Spectral clustering is then used to cluster the trajectories. Similarly, sparse subspace clustering [Elhamifar and Vidal, 2009] builds an affinity matrix by representing each trajectory as a sparse combination of all other trajectories and then applies spectral clustering on the resulting affinity matrix. Spectral clustering methods represent the state-of-the-art in motion segmentation. We believe this can be explained because the trajectories do not exactly form a linear subspace. Instead, such trajectories fall on a non-linear manifold.

With the realization of accurate trackers for dense long-term trajectories such as Sand and Teller [2008] and Sundaram et al. [2010] there has been great interest in exploiting dense long-term trajectories in motion segmentation. In particular, Brox and Malik [2010] achieve motion segmentation by creating an affinity matrix capturing similarity in translational motion across all pairs of trajectories. Spectral clustering is then used to oversegment the set of trajectories. A final grouping step then achieves motion segmentation. More recently, Fragkiadaki and Shi [2011] propose a two-step process that first uses trajectory saliency to segment foreground trajectories. This is followed by a two-stage spectral clustering of an affinity matrix computed over figure trajectories. The success of such approaches can be attributed in part to the large number of trajectories available. Such trajectories help capture the manifold structure empirically in the spectral clustering framework.

3.4 LAYERED-MOTION SEGMENTATION

Layered-motion segmentation refers to approaches that model the scene as a set of moving layers [Wang and Adelson, 1994]. Layers have a depth ordering, which, together with mattes and motion parameters, models how an image is generated. Figure 3.2 illustrates the concept of a layered model. Let n_l denote the number of layers, the i-th layer can be characterized by an appearance A_i, a motion map M_i, and a matte (also-called alpha map) L_i. To generate a frame at time t, the appearance of the i-th layer is first transformed according to the transformation parameters M_i^t using $f(A_i, L_i, M_i^t)$. The transformed appearances are then overlaid in the order specified by the depth of each layer d_i. Different variations are possible using different parameterizations of the variables or by including additional variables that describe, for example, lighting effects at each frame.

It is obvious that, if one knows the assignment of pixels to different segments, it is trivial to estimate the appearance and transformation parameters. Similarly, if one knows the appearance and transformation parameters, it is easy to assign pixels to segments. Since initially we know neither of them, this is an instance of a chicken-and-egg problem.

Wang and Adelson [1994] used an iterative method to achieve layered-motion segmentation. For every pair of frames they initialize using a set of motion models computed from square patches from the optical flow. Next, they iterate between assigning pixels to motion models and refining the motion models. This process is repeated until the number of pixel reassignments is less than a threshold or a maximum number of iterations is reached. Using the support maps for

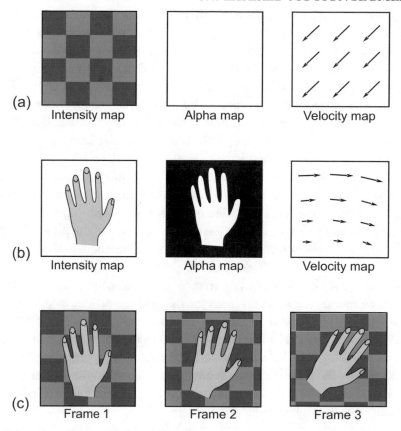

Figure 3.2: An illustration of the concept of layered-motion segmentation (adapted from Wang and Adelson [1994]) decomposition of a sequence to two layers. (a) The background layer: intensity map, matte (alpha map which is 1 everywhere), and motion map. (b) The foreground layer: intensity map, matte (1 at the foreground and 0 elsewhere), and motion map. (c) Synthesized image sequence based on the layers (courtesy of Edward H. Adelson. IEEE ©1994).

each segment, all pixels belonging to one segment are wrapped into a reference frame and combined using a median filter. A final counting step is used to establish depth ordering, based on the assumption that occluded pixels appear in fewer frames.

Mixture models were also used to probabilistically model the image-generation process. Mixture models have been used for optical flow computation earlier [Jepson and Black, 1993]. Weiss and Adelson [1996] used expectation maximization (EM) algorithms to update the model parameters. In the E-step, the system updates the conditional expectation of L_i given the fixed parameters. This is done by computing the residual of observed measurement and the predicted appearance given the motion parameters M_i^t. In the M-step, the model parameters A_i, M_i^t are up-dated based on these "soft" assignments. To incorporate spatial constraints in the mixture model, two methods were proposed. In the first, the images are pre-segmented based on static cues, and assignment in the E-step is based on the residual of all the pixels in each segment. In the second, a MRF prior is imposed on the labels L_i. The motion model of i-th layer is represented by the six parameters of an affine transformation. Although the approach reasons about occlusions by assigning pixels to the correct model, it does not infer the depth ordering of different layers.

Torr et al. [2001] extend the approach by modeling the layers as planes in 3D and inte-grating priors in a Bayesian framework. Both approaches rely on a key frame for estimation, and therefore can handle a few number of frames. Flexible sprites [Jojic and Frey, 2001] are another variation of layered-motion segmentation where transformations are restricted to a discrete set of predetermined transformations. A Gaussian model for pixel-wise appearance and mattes is used. A variational optimization is then used to learn the parameters of the probabilistic model. Most of these approaches either use expectation-maximization or variational inference to learn the model parameters.

Wills et al. [2003], noted the importance of spatial continuity prior to learning layered models. Given an initial estimate, they learn the shape of the regions using the α-expansion algo-rithm [Boykov et al., 1999], which guarantees a strong local minima. However, their method does not deal with multiple frames. Kumar et al. [2005] proposes a method that models spatial conti-nuity, while representing each layer as composed of a set of segments. Each segment is allowed to transform separately, thus enabling the method to handle nonrigid objects by segmenting them into multiple segments distributed over multiple layers. This flexibility comes at the expense of a less semantically meaningful representation.

A common theme of most layered models is the assumption that the video is available beforehand. Such assumption prevents the use of such approaches for processing videos from streaming sources. In addition, typically the computational complexity increases exponentially with the length of the videos.

3.5   MOTION-SEGMENTATION-BASED BACKGROUND-SUBTRACTION APPROACHES

Segmenting independent motions has been one of the traditional approaches for detection objects in video sequences. Most of the traditional approaches [e.g., Irani and Anandan, 1998, Irani et al., 1994, Odobez and Bouthemy, 1997] fit a motion model between two frames, e.g., affine motion, and independently moving objects are detected as outliers to the model fitting. However, these techniques do not maintain an appearance model of the scene background. In this section we focus on recent techniques [Elqursh and Elgammal, 2012, Kwak et al., 2011, Sheikh et al., 2009] that utilize motion segmentation to separate independent moving objects, and maintain a representation of the scene background. Interestingly, these recent techniques share a common feature, which is maintaining representations for both the background and the foreground.

3.5.1 ORTHOGRAPHIC CAMERA – FACTORIZATION-BASED BACKGROUND MODELS

Sheikh et al. [2009] used orthographic motion segmentation over a sliding window to segment a set of trajectories. This is followed by sparse per-frame appearance modeling, which is used later to obtain a dense image segmentation. The process starts with extracting point trajectories from a sequence of frames. These 2D trajectories are generated from various objects in the scene. Let $\mathbf{W}$ be the matrix formed by the set of all extracted trajectories. Assuming an affine camera, trajectories belonging to the stationary background will lie in a subspace of dimension three (as explained in Section 3.3). The next step is to identify which of these trajectories belong to the background subspace. Without additional assumptions, this problem is ill-posed, as there may exist other moving objects in the scene that also lie on a subspace of dimension three. To tackle this problem, it is assumed that the background subspace will contain the largest number of trajectories. This is reasonable only when objects in the scene do not span large areas of the image.

RANSAC [Fischler and Bolles, 1981] is used to extract the background subspace. RANSAC works in iterations, with each iteration consisting of a sampling step and a fitting step. In the sampling step, a set of three trajectories w_i, w_j, and w_k are sampled. The fitting step then measures the consensus, i.e., how many other trajectories fit the subspace identified by the sampled trajectories. Given the assumption that the background subspace will contain the largest number of trajectories, it is expected that when the sampled set of trajectories belongs to the background we get the largest consensus. The projection error on the subspace is used to measure the consensus. Given the RANSAC sample as a matrix of trajectories $\mathbf{W_S} = \begin{bmatrix} w_i & w_j & w_k \end{bmatrix}$, the projection matrix is constructed by

$$P = \mathbf{W}_S (\mathbf{W}_S^T \mathbf{W}_S)^{-1} \mathbf{W}_S^T .$$

The projection error can be written as $E_P(w_i) = \parallel \mathbf{P} w_i - w_i \parallel_2$. By comparing this error to a fixed threshold τ, the number of inlier trajectories can be determined. If we have low consensus, the process is repeated by sampling a new set of trajectories. Figure 3.3 illustrates an example of trajectory bases learned from a 30-frame time window, and examples of the foreground and background trajectories.

Motion segmentation using RANSAC into foreground and background trajectories gives only a sparse segmentation of the pixels in the frame. To achieve background subtraction, background and foreground appearance models are built using the sparse set of pixels belonging to the trajectories in the current frame. The algorithm labels the pixels in the current frame by maximizing the posterior of labeling given the set of sparsely labeled pixels. Let $\mathcal{L} = [l_1 \ldots l_N]$ denote the labels assigned to each pixel, and $x = [x_1 \ldots x_N]$ denote the spatial location and color of the pixels, the goal is to estimate

$$\mathcal{L}^* = arg \max_{\mathcal{L}} p(\mathcal{L}|x),$$

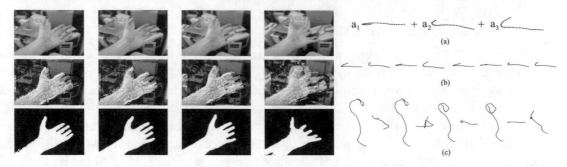

Figure 3.3: Left: Example results from Sheikh et al. [2009] Right: (a) The background trajectory bases of a 30-frame window. (b) Background trajectories lie in this subspace, (c) Foreground trajectories do not lie in this subspace (courtesy of Yaser Sheikh, IEEE ©2009).

$$p(\mathcal{L}|x) \propto p(\mathcal{L}) \prod_{i=1}^{N} p(x_i|l_i),$$

where the posterior is further factored using Bayes' Theorem into a prior and likelihood terms. The likelihood $p(x|\mathcal{L})$ is computed as

$$p(x_i|l_i) = p(x_i|\mathcal{B})^{(l_i-1)} p(x_i|\mathcal{F})^{l_i},$$

where $p(x_i|\mathcal{B})$ and $p(x_i|\mathcal{F})$ are the likelihood of a pixel given the background and foreground models, respectively. Kernel Density Estimation (KDE) was then used to model the appearance of the background and foreground from the sparse features' color and spatial locations (see Section 2.5 for details about KDE). Finally, a Markov Random Field was used to achieve the final labeling and enforce smoothness over the labels. Algorithm 1 illustrates a pseudocode for the Sheikh et al. [2009] approach.

Figure 3.3 shows an example of segmentation in a short sequence. More results can be seen in Figure 3.7. This method suffers from three drawbacks. The use of orthographic motion segmentation based on a sliding window means that motion information outside that window is lost. The fact that affine motion segmentation can only be applied on complete trajectories raises a trade-off. On one hand, increasing the window size captures more history, but at the cost of less trajectories. On the other hand, with a small window size more trajectories can be used at the cost of loss-of-motion history. In addition, the appearance models are built using sparse color information at the trajectory locations in the current frame and discarded after the frame is segmented. The sparse appearance modeling fails to capture object boundaries when appearance information is ambiguous. Due to the dependence on long-term trajectories only, regions with no trajectories may be disregarded as background altogether. Finally, the method fails if the assumption of orthographic projection is not satisfied.

Algorithm 1 Algorithm BSMC by Yasser Sheikh et al.

Sparse Labeling

    Track P points across F frames

    $t \leftarrow 0$

    while $t < T$ **do**

        Randomly select 3 trajectories $\begin{bmatrix} w_i, & w_j, & w_k \end{bmatrix}$

        Compute a projection matrix P

        Find inlier trajectories $\{w_l\}$

        if $l > d$ **then**

            Break

        end if

        $t \leftarrow t + 1$

    end while

Pixel–wise Labeling

    Create background model ψ_b from inliers

    Create foreground model ψ_f from inliers

    for i=1 to N **do**

        Compute $p(x_i|\psi_f)$ and $p(x_i|\psi_b)$

    end for

    Maximize a posterior using likelihoods $p(x_i|\psi_f)$ and $p(x_i|\psi_b)$, with an MRF prior using graph cuts.

3.5.2   DENSE BAYESIAN APPEARANCE MODELING

Maintaining the background and foreground appearance representation at the level of sparse features in Sheikh et al. [2009] results in arbitrary segmentation boundaries at the dense segmentation, at areas where there are not many tracked features (e.g., see Figure 3.7). In contrast, recent approaches like Kwak et al. [2011] and Elqursh and Elgammal [2012] maintain a dense appearance representation at the block level in Kwak et al. [2011] and at the pixel level in Elqursh and Elgammal [2012]. Both approaches uses a Baysian filtering framework, where the appearance representation from the previous frame is considered as a prior model, which is propagated to the current frame using a motion model to obtain the appearance posterior. We explain the details of these two approaches next.

    Kwak et al. [2011] proposed a method that maintains block-based appearance models for the background and foreground within a Bayesian filtering framework. Optical flow is computed and used to robustly estimate motion by non-parametric belief propagation in a Markov Random Field. Figure 3.4 illustrates the approach. To update the appearance models, the method iterates between estimating the motion of the blocks and inferring the labels of the pixels. Once converged, the appearance models are used as priors for the next frame and the process continues.

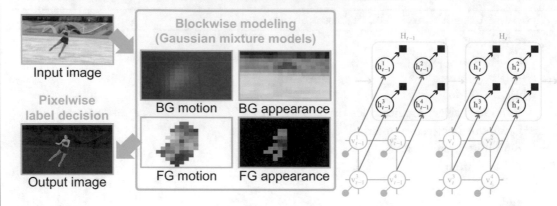

Figure 3.4: Left: Illustration of the approach of Kwak et al. [2011]. A block-based appearance and motion representations are maintained for the background and foreground layers. Right: A graphical model for the approach, where an MRF over the blocks is used, the random variables v's indicate the motion and h's indicate the color appearance (courtesy of Bohyung Han, IEEE ©2011).

Due to the iterative nature of the approach, the method is susceptible to reach a local minimum. Although motion information between successive frames is estimated, it is only used to estimate the labels in the current frame and does not carry on to future frames. In contrast, Elqursh and Elgammal [2012] maintained motion information via long-term trajectories and used Bayesian filtering to maintain the belief over different labelings.

3.5.3   MOVING AWAY FROM THE AFFINE ASSUMPTION – MANIFOLD-BASED BACKGROUND MODELS

One way to avoid the trade-off caused by the affine motion-segmentation model, as in Sheikh et al. [2009], is to attempt to use an alternative method for motion segmentation. Elqursh and Elgammal [2013] showed that, in the general perspective case, the projection of 3D trajectories to 2D image coordinates forms a three-dimensional manifold. Elqursh and Elgammal [2013] proposed an online motion segmentation approach based on an online version of label propagation. Earlier, Elqursh and Elgammal [2012] proposed to use nonlinear manifold embedding to achieve online motion segmentation into foreground and background clusters. This approach moves away from traditional affine factorization and formulates the motion segmentation as a manifold separation problem. This approach is online, with constant computation per frame, and does not depend on a sliding window, in contrast long-term trajectory information are utilized. The approach can be seen as a layered-motion segmentation one, however, in contrast to the methods described in Section 3.4, which are mainly offline, this approach is online.

Moreover, in contrast to the previous methods, where the motion segmentation output was used directly to model the appearance, the result of the motion segmentation is used to build

Figure 3.5: Illustration of the Elqursh and Elgammal [2012] approach. Left: Graphical model. Center: Automatic segmentation obtained on long sequence with fast articulated motion. The method is able to segment the tennis ball even when no trajectories exist on it. Right: One sample from the background pixel based appearance model learned automatically (Springer ©2012).

dense motion models $\mathcal{M} = (\mathbf{M}_f, \mathbf{M}_b)$ for the foreground and background layers respectively. These motion models, together with the input frame I_t are used to update pixel-level appearance models $\mathcal{A} = \{A_b, A_f\}$ computed from the previous frame in a Bayesian tracking framework. The process is then repeated for each incoming frame. Figure 3.5 illustrates the graphical model for the approach and an example of the foreground segmentation and background model learned. Algorithm 2 summarizes the algorithm.

To perform the motion segmentation, for all pairs of trajectories a distance matrix is computed $\mathbf{D}_t$ and an affinity matrix $\mathbf{W}_t$ is formed. The distance between trajectories does not require that the trajectories should have the same length. A multi-step approach is then used to achieve motion segmentation. First, Laplacian Eigenmaps [Belkin and Niyogi, 2003] is applied to compute a low-dimensional representation of the trajectories. Then a Gaussian Mixture Model (GMM) is used to cluster the set of trajectories. To initialize the clustering, the labels of the trajectories from the previous frame $\mathbf{c}_{t-1}$ is used. Figure 3.6 shows an example of such a clustering in the embedding coordinates. A final grouping step based on several cues is used to merge the clusters into exactly two sets; namely a foreground manifold and background manifold.

Output of the motion segmentation is used to compute the motion models. Each motion model $\mathbf{M}$ is a grid of motion vectors $\mathbf{m}^i = [u_i v_i]$, where u_i, and v_i denote the motion of pixel i in the x and y directions respectively. The motion segmentation result gives motion information and layer assignments at a subset of the pixels (albeit with some noise in the motion due to tracking). To propagate this information over all pixels and layers, Gaussian belief propagation (GBP) is used. The result is the marginal distribution of the motion at each pixel and is represented by a mean and variance.

Assuming that the previous appearance models are provided, the approach then computes the predicted appearance models $\mathcal{A}_t = \{A_{b,t}, A_{f,t}\}$ and labels $L_t = \{l_t^i\}$. The models are again represented as a grid of pixel-wise representation a_b^i, a_f^i, and l^i where a_b^i, a_f^i, l^i denote the color

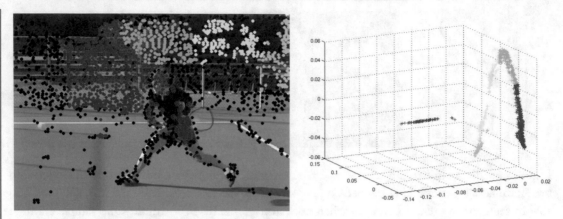

Figure 3.6: Example trajectories in the image and their corresponding embedding coordinates, from Elqursh and Elgammal [2012]. Each cluster is marked with a different color. Black dots are short trajectories not yet added to the embedding. The foreground cluster is marked with two red concentric circles around its trajectories (Springer ©2012).

in background, color in foreground, and label of pixel i. To simplify the notation we drop the subscript denoting the layer assignment when the equation applies to all layers. Prediction then follows

$$p(a_t^i) = \sum_{m_t^i \in \mathbb{N}^2} p(m_t^i) p(a_{t-1}^j), \tag{3.3}$$

$$p(l_t^i = f) = \sum_{m_{f,t}^i \in \mathbb{N}^2} p(m_f^i) p(l_{t-1}^j = f), \tag{3.4}$$

where j is the pixel m_f^i units away from pixel i. The distribution $p(a^i)$ is approximated using kernel density estimation as a set of N_{KDE} color samples. In the update step, the new frame I_t is incorporated. Given the predicted label priors and appearance models, a MAP estimate of the labels is inferred using the equation

$$p(l_t^i = k | I_t^i) \propto \int_{a_k^i} p(I_t^i | l_t^i, a_{k,t}^i) p(a_{k,t}^i) \, \mathbf{d}a_{k,t}^i \, p(l_t^i). \tag{3.5}$$

Next, the inferred labels are used to update the corresponding appearance model. This is done by adding the observed pixel color I_t^i to the set KDE samples of pixel i in the foreground layer if $p(l_t^i = f | I_t^i) > \frac{1}{2}$ and to the background otherwise. Algorithm 2 illustrates a pseudocode for the Elqursh and Elgammal [2012] approach.

Figure 3.7 shows qualitative comparisons between Elqursh and Elgammal [2012] and Sheikh et al. [2009] on three sequences. Notice that the dense segmentation of Sheikh et al. [2009] erroneously extends around the foreground in areas where there are no tracked features. This is due to the modeling the appearance at the sparse tracked features, as described above. Also notice that, when the orthographic camera assumption in Sheikh et al. [2009] fails, as in the third case, the resulting segmentation is totally erroneous. In contrast the approach in Elqursh and Elgammal [2012] does not have such an assumption and accurately detects and segments targets in these situations.

Algorithm 2 BSMC using nonlinear manifold segmentation and appearance modeling [Elqursh and Elgammal, 2012]

Input: Images $I_1, I_2, \ldots$ and trajectories $W_1, W_2, \ldots$, Output pixel labeling at $\mathbf{L}_1, \mathbf{L}_2, \ldots$ Algorithm:

    for t = 1 to K **do**

        Perform initialization, compute $(\mathbf{c}_K, \mathbf{D}_K, \mathcal{A}_K, \mathbf{L}_K)$

    end for

    while frame t exist(i.e., received $\mathbf{I}_t$) **do**

        Update motion segmentation

        $\mathbf{D}_t = \max(\mathbf{D_{t-1}}, \mathbf{D_{t-1:t}})$, $\mathbf{W}_t = exp(-\mathbf{D}_t/\lambda)$

        Compute embedding coordinates $\mathbf{X}_t = laplacian-eigenmaps(\mathbf{W}_t)$

        Apply GMM using $\mathbf{c}_{t-1}$ for initialization.

        Label each cluster foreground/background using several cues.

        Estimate dense motion model $\mathbf{M}_f$, and $\mathbf{M}_b$.

        Predict the appearance $\mathcal{A}_{t|t-1}$ and labels $\mathbf{L}_{t|t-1}$ given $\mathbf{M_b}, \mathbf{M_f}$

        Update $\mathbf{L}_t$ given $\mathcal{A}_{t|t-1}$ and $\mathbf{I}_t$

        Update appearance models $\mathcal{A}_t = (\mathbf{A}_f, \mathbf{A}_b)$

        $t = t + 1$

    end while

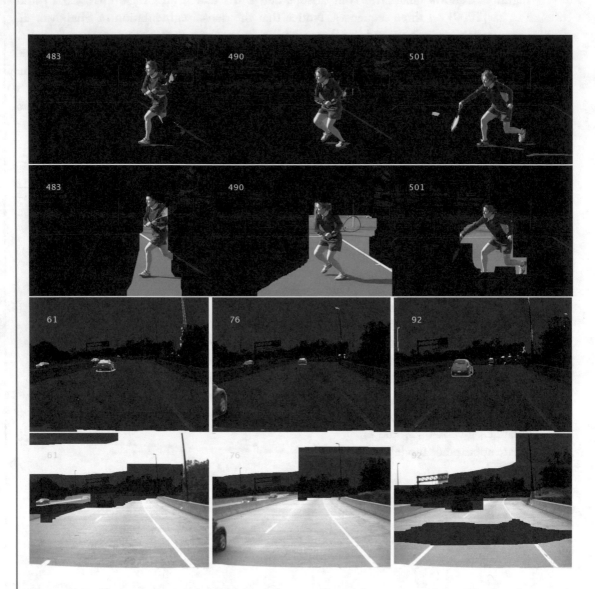

Figure 3.7: Comparative results on three sequences. For each sequence, the top frames show results of Elqursh and Elgammal [2012] and the bottom frames show the results of Sheikh et al. [2009]. For visualization purposes, background regions are darkened while foreground regions maintain their colors (best viewed in color) (Springer ©2012).

Bibliography

Shoichi Araki, Takashi Matsuoka, Naokazu Yokoya, and Haruo Takemura. Real-time tracking of multiple moving object contours in a moving camera image sequence. *IEICE Transactions on Information and Systems*, 83(7):1583–1591, 2000. DOI: 10.1109/ICPR.1998.711972. 40

Mikhail Belkin and Partha Niyogi. Laplacian Eigenmaps for Dimensionality Reduction and Data Representation. *Neural Computation*, 1396:1373–1396, 2003. DOI: 10.1162/089976603321780317. 51

Thierry Bouwmans, Fida El Baf, and Bertrand Vachon. Background modeling using mixture of gaussians for foreground detection-a survey. *Recent Patents on Computer Science*, 1(3):219–237, 2008. DOI: 10.2174/2213275910801030219. 18

Yuri Boykov, Olga Veksler, and Ramin Zabih. Fast Approximate Energy Minimization via Graph Cuts. In *Proc. of the Seventh IEEE International Conference on Computer Vision*, pages 377–384 vol.1. IEEE, 1999. ISBN 0-7695-0164-8. doi: 10.1109/ICCV.1999.791245. http://ieeexplore.ieee.org/lpdocs/epic03/wrapper.htm?arnumber=791245. DOI: 10.1109/ICCV.1999.791245. 46

Thomas Brox and Jitendra Malik. Object Segmentation by Long Term Analysis of Point Trajectories. In *Proc. of the 11th European Conference on Computer Vision*, pages 282–295, 2010. DOI: 10.1007/978-3-642-15555-0_21. 43, 44

Serhat S. Bucak and Bilge Gunsel. Incremental subspace learning via non-negative matrix factorization. *Pattern Recognition*, 42(5):788–797, May 2009. ISSN 0031-3203. DOI: 10.1016/j.patcog.2008.09.002. 26

Wilhelm Burger and Mark Burge. *Digital Image Processing, an Algorithmic Introduction Using Java*. Springer, 2008. 28

Yizong Cheng. Mean shift, mode seeking, and clustering. *IEEE Transaction on Pattern Analysis and Machine Intelligence*, 17(8):790–799, Aug 1995. DOI: 10.1109/34.400568. 22

Dorin Comaniciu. *Nonparametric Robust Methods For Computer Vision*. PhD thesis, Rutgers, The State University of New Jersey, January 2000. 19

Dorin Comaniciu and Peter Meer. Mean shift analysis and applications. In *Proc. of the 7th IEEE International Conference on Computer Vision*, volume 2, pages 1197–1203, Sep 1999. DOI: 10.1109/ICCV.1999.790416. 22

João Costeira and Takeo Kanade. A Multi-body Factorization Method for Motion Analysis. In *Proc. of the 5th IEEE International Conference on Computer Vision*, pages 1071–1076. IEEE Comput. Soc. Press, 1995. ISBN 0-8186-7042-8. doi: 10.1109/ICCV .1995.466815. http://ieeexplore.ieee.org/lpdocs/epic03/wrapper.htm?arnumber =466815. DOI: 10.1109/ICCV.1995.466815. 42, 43

Rita Cucchiara, Costantino Grana, Massimo Piccardi, and Andrea Prati. Detecting moving objects, ghosts, and shadows in video streams. *IEEE Transactions on Pattern Analysis and Machine Intelligence*, 25:1337–1342, 2003. DOI: 10.1109/TPAMI.2003.1233909. 27, 29

Navneet Dalal and Bill Triggs. Histograms of oriented gradients for human detection. In *Proc. of the IEEE Computer Society Conference on Computer Vision and Pattern Recognition*, 2005. DOI: 10.1109/CVPR.2005.177. 5, 10

Thomas Dean, Mark A Ruzon, Mark Segal, Jonathon Shlens, Sudheendra Vijayanarasimhan, and Jay Yagnik. Fast, accurate detection of 100,000 object classes on a single machine. In *Proc. of the IEEE Computer Society Conference on Conference on Computer Vision and Pattern Recognition*, 2013. DOI: 10.1109/CVPR.2013.237. 7

Daniel DeMenthon and Remi Megret. D DeMenthon and R Megret. Spatio-temporal segmentation of video by hierarchical mean shift analysis. In *Workshop Statistical Methods in Video Processing*, 2002. 7

Arthur P. Dempster, Nan M. Laird, and Donald B. Rubin. Maximum likelihood from incomplete data via the em algorithm. *Journal of the Royal Statistical Society*, 39:1–38, 1977. 16

Piotr Dollár, Christian Wojek, Bernt Schiele, and Pietro Perona. Pedestrian detection: A benchmark. In *Proc. of the IEEE Computer Society Conference on Computer Vision and Pattern Recognition*, pages 304–311, 2009. DOI: 10.1109/CVPRW.2009.5206631. 6

G. W. Donohoe, Don R. Hush, and Nasir Ahmed. change detection for target detection and classification in video sequences. In *Proc. of the International Conference on Acoustics, Speech and Signal Processing*, 1988. DOI: 10.1109/ICASSP.1988.196783. 16

Richard O. Duda, David G. Stork, and Peter E. Hart. *Pattern Classification*. Wiley, John & Sons,, 2000. 18, 19, 21

Hassan J. Eghbali. K-s test for detecting changes from landsat imagery data. *IEEE Transactions on Systems, Man and Cybernetics*, 9(1):17–23, 1979. 8

Ahmed Elgammal. *Efficient Kernel Density Estimation for Realtime Computer Vision*. PhD thesis, University of Maryland, 2002. 18, 19, 20, 21

Ahmed Elgammal, David Harwood, and Larry S. Davis. Nonparametric background model for background subtraction. In *Proc. of the 6th European Conference of Computer Vision*, 2000. DOI: 10.1007/3-540-45053-X_48. 10, 11, 13, 18, 20, 21, 22, 27, 28, 29, 30, 31, 32, 35

Ahmed Elgammal, Ramani Duraiswami, and Larry S. Davis. Efficient non-parametric adaptive color modeling using fast gauss transform. In *Proc. of the IEEE Computer Society Conference on Computer Vision and Pattern Recognition*, 2001. DOI: 10.1109/CVPR.2001.991012. 23

Ehsan Elhamifar and René Vidal. Sparse subspace clustering. In *Proc. of the IEEE Computer Society Conference on Computer Vision and Pattern Recognition*, pages 2790–2797, 2009. ISBN 978-1-4244-3992-8. doi: 10.1109/CVPR.2009.5206547. http://ieeexplore.ieee.org/lpdocs/epic03/wrapper.htm?arnumber=5206547. DOI: 10.1109/CVPR.2009.5206547. 44

Ali Elqursh and Ahmed Elgammal. Online moving camera background subtraction. In *Proc. of the 12th European Conference of Computer Vision, 2012*, pages 228–241. Springer, 2012. DOI: 10.1007/978-3-642-33783-3_17. 46, 49, 50, 51, 52, 53, 54

Ali Elqursh and Ahmed Elgammal. Online motion segmentation using dynamic label propagation. In *Proc. of the International Conference on Computer Vision*, 2013. DOI: 10.1109/ICCV.2013.251. 50

Pedro F. Felzenszwalb and Daniel P. Huttenlocher. Pictorial structures for object recognition. *International Journal of Computer Vision*, 61(1):55–79, 2005. DOI: 10.1023/B:VISI.0000042934.15159.49. 6

Pedro F Felzenszwalb, Ross B Girshick, David McAllester, and Deva Ramanan. Object detection with discriminatively trained part-based models. *IEEE Transactions on Pattern Analysis and Machine Intelligence*, 32(9):1627–1645, 2010. DOI: 10.1109/TPAMI.2009.167. 6

Martin A Fischler and Robert C Bolles. Random sample consensus: a paradigm for model fitting with applications to image analysis and automated cartography. *Commun. ACM*, 24(6):381–395, June 1981. ISSN 0001-0782. doi: 10.1145/358669.358692. http://dx.doi.org/10.1145/358669.358692. DOI: 10.1145/358669.358692. 39, 43, 47

Charless Fowlkes, Serge Belongie, Fan Chung, and Jitendra Malik. Spectral grouping using the Nystrom method. *IEEE Transactions on Pattern Analaysis and Machine Intelligence*, 2004. DOI: 10.1109/TPAMI.2004.1262185. 7

Katerina Fragkiadaki and Jianbo Shi. Detection Free Tracking: Exploiting Motion and Topology for Segmenting and Tracking under Entanglement. In *Proc. of the IEEE Computer Society Conference on Computer Vision and Pattern Recognition*, pages 2073–2080, 2011. ISBN 978-1-4577-0394-2. doi: 10.1109/CVPR.2011.5995366. http://ieeexplore.ieee.org/lpdocs/epic03/wrapper.htm?arnumber=5995366. DOI: 10.1109/CVPR.2011.5995366. 44

Nir Friedman and Stuart Russell. Image segmentation in video sequences: A probabilistic approach. In *Uncertainty in Artificial Intelligence*, 1997. 16

Keinosuke Fukunaga and Larry Hostetler. The estimation of the gradient of a density function, with application in pattern recognition. *IEEE Transaction on Information Theory*, 21:32–40, 1975. DOI: 10.1109/TIT.1975.1055330. 22

Xiang Gao, Terrance E. Boult, Frans Coetzee, and Visvanathan Ramesh. Error analysis of background adaption. In *Proc. of the IEEE Computer Society Conference on Computer Vision and Pattern Recognition*, 2000. DOI: 10.1109/CVPR.2000.855861. 16, 18

Dariu M Gavrila. Pedestrian detection from a moving vehicle. In *Proc. of the 6th European Conference of Computer Vision*, 2000 pages 37–49. Springer, 2000. DOI: 10.1007/3-540-45053-X_3. 5

Hayit Greenspan, Jacob Goldberger, and Arnaldo Mayer. A Probabilistic Framework for Spatio-Temporal Video Representation & Indexing. In *Proc. of the 7th European Conference on Computer Vision*, 2002. DOI: 10.1007/3-540-47979-1_31. 7

Amit Gruber and Yair Weiss. Multibody factorization with uncertainty and missing data using the EM algorithm. In *Proc. of the IEEE Computer Society Conference on Computer Vision and Pattern Recognition*, volume 1, pages 707–714, 2004. ISBN 0-7695-2158-4. doi: 10.1109/CVPR.2004.1315101. http://ieeexplore.ieee.org/lpdocs/epic03/wrapper.htm?arnumber=1315101. DOI: 10.1109/CVPR.2004.1315101. 43

André Guéziec. Tracking pitches for broadcast television. *Computer*, 35(3):38–43, March 2002. ISSN 0018-9162. DOI: 10.1109/2.989928. 10

Ernest L. Hall. *Computer Image Processing and Recognition*. Academic Press, 1979. 29

Bohyung Han, Durin Comaniciu, and Larry Davis. Sequential kernel density approximation through mode propagation: Applications to background modeling. In *Proc. of the Asian Conference on Computer Vision*, 2004. 22

Ismail Haritaoglu, David Harwood, and Larry S. Davis. W4:who? when? where? what? a real time system for detecting and tracking people. In *Proc. of the International Conference on Face and Gesture Recognition*, 1998. DOI: 10.1109/CVPR.1998.698720. 10

Richard I. Hartley and Andrew Zisserman. *Multiple View Geometry in Computer Vision*. Cambridge University Press, ISBN: 0521540518, second edition, 2004. DOI: 10.1017/CBO9780511811685. 39, 42

Michael Harville. A framework for high-level feedback to adaptive, per-pixel, mixture-of-gaussian background models. In *Proc. of the 7th European Conference of Computer Vision*, pages 543–560, 2002. DOI: 10.1007/3-540-47977-5_36. 17

Eric Hayman and Jan olof Eklundh. Statistical background subtraction for a mobile observer. In *Proc. of the 9th International Conference on Computer Vision*, pages 67–74, 2003. DOI: 10.1109/ICCV.2003.1238315. 40, 41

Thanarat Horprasert, David Harwood, and Larry S. Davis. A statistical approach for real-time robust background subtraction and shadow detection. In *IEEE Frame-Rate Applications Workshop*, 1999. 27, 29, 30, 31, 33

Thanarat Horprasert, David Harwood, and Larry S Davis. A robust background subtraction and shadow detection. In *Proc. of the Asian Conference on Computer Vision*, pages 983–988, 2000. 30, 31, 33

Y. Z. Hsu, H. H. Nagel, and G. Rekers. New likelihood test methods for change detection in image sequences. *Computer Vision and Image Processing*, 26:73–106, 1984. DOI: 10.1016/0734-189X(84)90131-2. 26

Ivan Huerta, Michael Holte, Thomas Moeslund, and Jordi Gonzàlez. Detection and removal of chromatic moving shadows in surveillance scenarios. In *Proc. of the 12th International Conference on Computer Vision*, pages 1499–1506, 2009. DOI: 10.1109/ICCV.2009.5459280. 26, 28, 29, 30, 31, 32, 34

Ivan Huerta, Ariel Amato, Xavier Roca, and Jordi Gonzàlez. Exploiting multiple cues in motion segmentation based on background subtraction. *Neurocomputing*, 100(0):183 – 196, 2013. ISSN 0925-2312. doi: http://dx.doi.org/10.1016/j.neucom.2011.10.036. http://www.sciencedirect.com/science/article/pii/S092523121200330X. Special issue: Behaviours in video. DOI: 10.1016/j.neucom.2011.10.036. 31, 32

Naoyuki Ichimura. Motion Segmentation Based on Factorization Method and Discriminant Criterion. In *Proc. of the 7th International Conference on Computer Vision*, 1999. DOI: 10.1109/ICCV.1999.791279. 43

Michal Irani and P Anandan. A unified approach to moving object detection in 2d and 3d scenes. *IEEE Transactions on Pattern Analysis and Machine Intelligence*, 20(6):577–589, 1998. DOI: 10.1109/34.683770. 7, 46

Michal Irani, Benny Rousso, and Shmuel Peleg. Computing occluding and transparent motions. *International Journal of Computer Vision*, 12(1):5–16, February 1994. ISSN 0920-5691. doi: 10.1007/BF01420982. http://www.springerlink.com/content/h560577x56012443/. DOI: 10.1007/BF01420982. 7, 46

Sumer Jabri, Zoran Duric, Harry Wechsler, and Azriel Rosenfeld. Detection and location of people in video images using adaptive fusion of color and edge information. In *Proc. of the International Conference of Pattern Recognition*, 2000. DOI: 10.1109/ICPR.2000.902997. 26, 31

Ramesh C. Jain and H.H. Nagel. On the analysis of accumulative difference pictures from image sequences of real world scenes. *IEEE Transaction on Pattern Analysis and Machine Intelligence*, 1(2):206–213, April 1979. DOI: 10.1109/TPAMI.1979.4766907. 8

Vidit Jain and Erik Learned-Miller. Online Domain Adaptation of a Pre-Trained Cascade of Classifiers. In *Proc. of the IEEE Computer Society Conference on Computer Vision and Pattern Recognition*, pages 577–584. IEEE, June 2011. ISBN 978-1-4577-0394-2. doi: 10.1109/CVPR.2011.5995317. http://ieeexplore.ieee.org/lpdocs/epic03/wrapper.htm?arnumber=5995317. DOI: 10.1109/CVPR.2011.5995317. 6

Omar Javed, Khurram Shafique, and Mubarak Shah. A hierarchical approach to robust background subtraction using color and gradient information. In *IEEE Workshop on Motion and Video Computing*, pages 22–27, 2002. DOI: 10.1109/MOTION.2002.1182209. 17

Allan Jepson and Michael J. Black. Mixture Models for Optical Flow Computation. In *Proc. of the IEEE Computer Society Conference on Computer Vision and Pattern Recognition*, pages 760–761, 1993. IEEE Comput. Soc. Press, 1993. ISBN 0-8186-3880-X. doi: 10.1109/CVPR.1993.341161. http://ieeexplore.ieee.org/lpdocs/epic03/wrapper.htm?arnumber=341161. DOI: 10.1109/CVPR.1993.341161. 45

Yuxin Jin, Linmi Tao, Huijun Di, Naveed I Rao, and Guangyou Xu. Background modeling from a free-moving camera by multi-layer homography algorithm. In *Proc. of the 15th IEEE International Conference on Image Processing*, pages 1572–1575. IEEE, 2008. DOI: 10.1109/ICIP.2008.4712069. 40

Gunnar Johansson. *Configurations in event perception*. PhD thesis, 1950. 5

Gunnar Johansson. Visual perception of biological motion and a model for its analysis. *Perception & psychophysics*, 14(2):201–211, 1973. DOI: 10.3758/BF03212378. 5

Nebojsa Jojic and Brendan J. Frey. Learning Flexible Sprites in Video Layers. In *Proc. of the IEEE Computer Society Conference on Computer Vision and Pattern Recognition*, pages I–199–I–206. IEEE Comput. Soc, 2001. ISBN 0-7695-1272-0. doi: 10.1109/CVPR.2001.990476. http://ieeexplore.ieee.org/lpdocs/epic03/wrapper.htm?arnumber=990476. DOI: 10.1109/CVPR.2001.990476. 46

Rudolph Emil Kalman. A new approach to linear filtering and prediction problems. *Journal of Basic Engineering*, 82(1):35–45, 1960. DOI: 10.1115/1.3662552. 10, 23

Ken-Ichi Kanatani. Camera rotation invariance of image characteristics. *Computer vision, graphics, and image processing*, 39(3):328–354, 1987. DOI: 10.1016/S0734-189X(87)80185-8. 40

Ken-Ichi Kanatani. Motion Segmentation by Subspace Separation and Model Selection. In *Proc. of the 8th International Conference on Computer Vision*, volume 2, pages 586–591. IEEE,

2001. ISBN 0769511430101. http://ieeexplore.ieee.org/xpls/abs_all.jsp?arnum ber=937679. DOI: 10.1109/ICCV.2001.937679. 43

Klaus-Peter Karmann and Achim von Brandt. Moving object recognition using adaptive back-ground memory. In *Time-Varying Image Processing and Moving Object Recognition*. Elsevier Science Publishers B.V., 1990. 16, 23, 32, 34

Klaus-Peter Karmann, Achim V. Brandt, and Rainer Gerl. Moving object segmentation based on adaptive reference images. In *Signal Processing V: Theories and Application*. Elsevier Science Publishers B.V., 1990. 16, 23

Kyungnam Kim, Thanarat H. Chalidabhongse, David Harwood, and Larry Davis. Background modeling and subtraction by codebook construction. In *Proc. of the International Conference on Image Processing*, pages 3061–3064, 2004. DOI: 10.1109/ICIP.2004.1421759. 29

Kyungnam Kim, David Harwood, and Larry S. Davis. Background updating for visual surveil-lance. In *Proc. of the International Symposium on Visual Computing*, pages 1–337, 2005. DOI: 10.1007/11595755_41. 36

Asanobu Kitamoto. The moments of the mixel distribution and its application to statistical im-age classification. In *Advances in Pattern Recognition*, pages 521–531. Springer, 2000. DOI: 10.1007/3-540-44522-6_54. 41

D. Koller, J. Weber, T.Huang, J.Malik, G. Ogasawara, B.Rao, and S.Russell. Towards robust automatic traffic scene analyis in real-time. In *Proc. of the International Conference of Pattern Recognition*, 1994. DOI: 10.1109/ICPR.1994.576243. 16, 23, 32

M. Pawan Kumar, Philip HS. Torr, and Andrew Zisserman. Learning Layered Motion Seg-mentations of Video. *Proc. of the 10th International Conference on Computer Vision*, (iii), 2005. DOI: 10.1007/s11263-007-0064-x. 46

Suha Kwak, Taegyu Lim, Woonhyun Nam, Bohyung Han, and Joon Hee Han. General-ized Background Subtraction Based on Hybrid Inference by Belief Propagation and Bayesian Filtering. In *Proc. of the 13th International Conference on Computer Vision*, 2011. DOI: 10.1109/ICCV.2011.6126494. 46, 49, 50

Martin D. Levine. *Vision in Man and Machine*. McGraw-Hill Book Company, 1985. 28

Yongmin Li. On incremental and robust subspace learning. *Pattern recognition*, 37(7):1509–1518, 2004. DOI: 10.1016/j.patcog.2003.11.010. 25

Lucia Maddalena and Alfredo Petrosino. A self-organizing approach to background subtraction for visual surveillance applications. *IEEE Transactions on Image Processing*, 17(7):1168–1177, July 2008. DOI: 10.1109/TIP.2008.924285. 26

T. Matsuyama, Takashi Ohya, and Hitoshi Habe. Background subtraction for nonstationary scenes. In *4th Asian Conference on Computer Vision*, 2000. 26

Stephen J. Mckenna, Sumer Jabri, Zoran Duric, Harry Wechsler, and Azriel Rosenfeld. Tracking groups of people. *Computer Vision and Image Understanding*, 80:42–56, 2000. DOI: 10.1006/cviu.2000.0870. 26, 31

Anurag Mittal and Dan Huttenlocher. Scene modeling for wide area surveillance and image synthesis. In *Proc. of the IEEE Computer Society Conference on Computer Vision and Pattern Recognition*, 2000. DOI: 10.1109/CVPR.2000.854767. 18, 40, 41

Anurag Mittal and Nikos Paragios. Motion-based background subtraction using adaptive kernel density estimation. In *Proc. of the IEEE Computer Society Conference on Computer Vision and Pattern Recognition*, pages 302–309, 2004. DOI: 10.1109/CVPR.2004.1315179. 22, 26, 32

Joseph L. Mundy and Andrew Zisserman, editors. *Geometric Invariance in Computer Vision*. MIT Press, Cambridge, MA, USA, 1992. ISBN 0-262-13285-0. 42

Don Murray and Anup Basu. Motion tracking with an active camera. *IEEE Transactions on Pattern Analysis and Machine Intelligence*, 16(5):449–459, 1994. DOI: 10.1109/34.291452. 39, 40

Radford M. Neal and Geoffrey E. Hinton. A new view of the em algorithm that justifies incremental and other variants. In *Learning in Graphical Models*, pages 355–368. Kluwer Academic Publishers, 1993. 16

Peter Ochs and Thomas Brox. Higher order motion models and spectral clustering. In *Proc. of the IEEE Computer Society Conference on Computer Vision and Pattern Recognition*, pages 614–621, 2012. ISBN 978-1-4673-1228-8. doi: 10.1109/CVPR.2012.6247728. http://ieeexplore.ieee.org/lpdocs/epic03/wrapper.htm?arnumber=6247728. DOI: 10.1109/CVPR.2012.6247728. 43

JM Odobez and P Bouthemy. Separation of moving regions from background in an image sequence acquired with a mobil camera. In *Video Data Compression for Multimedia Computing*, pages 283–311. Springer, 1997. DOI: 10.1007/978-1-4615-6239-9_8. 7, 46

Nuria M Oliver, Barbara Rosario, and Alex P Pentland. A bayesian computer vision system for modeling human interactions. , *IEEE Transactions on Pattern Analysis and Machine Intelligence*, 22(8):831–843, 2000. DOI: 10.1109/34.868684. 25

Michael Oren, Constantine Papageorgiou, Pawan Sinha, Edgar Osuna, and Tomaso Poggio. Pedestrian detection using wavelet templates. In *Proc. of the IEEE Computer Society Conference on Computer Vision and Pattern Recognition*, pages 193–199, 1997. DOI: 10.1109/CVPR.1997.609319. 5

Toufiq Parag, Ahmed Elgammal, and Anurag Mittal. A framework for feature selection for background subtraction. In *Proc. of the IEEE Computer Society Conference on Computer Vision and Pattern Recognition*, 2006. DOI: 10.1109/CVPR.2006.24. 22, 23, 26

Kedar Patwardhan, Guillermo Sapiro, and Vassilios Morellas. Robust foreground detection in video using pixel layers. *IEEE Transaction on Pattern Analysis and Machine Intelligence*, 30: 746–751, April 2008. ISSN 0162-8828. doi: 10.1109/TPAMI.2007.70843. http://portal .acm.org/citation.cfm?id=1345870.1345959. DOI: 10.1109/TPAMI.2007.70843. 23

Mary A Peterson and Bradley S Gibson. The initial identification of figure-ground relationships: Contributions from shape recognition processes. *Bulletin of the Psychonomic Society*, 29(3):199–202, 1991. DOI: 10.3758/BF03342677. 5

Massimo Piccardi and Tony Jan. Mean-shift background image modelling. In *Proc. of the International Conference on Image Processing*, pages V: 3399–3402, 2004. DOI: 10.1109/ICIP.2004.1421844. 22

Ying Ren, Chin-Seng Chua, and Yeong-Khing Ho. Statistical background modeling for non-stationary camera. *Pattern Recognition Letter*, 24(1-3):183–196, 2003. ISSN 0167-8655. DOI: 10.1016/S0167-8655(02)00210-6. 41

Jens Rittscher, Jien Kato, Sébastien Joga, and Andrew Blake. A probabilistic background model for tracking. In *Proc. of the 6th European Conference on Computer Vision*, 2000. DOI: 10.1007/3-540-45053-X_22. 24

Simon Rowe and Andrew Blake. Statistical mosaics for tracking. *Image and Vision Computing*, 14(8):549–564, 1996. DOI: 10.1016/0262-8856(96)01103-1. 16, 40

J Rymel, J Renno, Darrel Greenhill, James Orwell, and Graeme A. Jones. Adaptive eigen-backgrounds for object detection. In *Proc. of the International Conference on Image Processing*, volume 3, pages 1847–1850. IEEE, 2004. DOI: 10.1109/ICIP.2004.1421436. 25

Peter Sand and Seth Teller. Particle Video: Long-Range Motion Estimation Using Point Trajectories. *International Journal of Computer Vision*, 80(1):72–91, May 2008. ISSN 0920-5691. doi: 10.1007/s11263-008-0136-6. http://www.springerlink.com/index/10.1007/s11263-008-0136-6. DOI: 10.1007/s11263-008-0136-6. 44

David W. Scott. *Mulivariate Density Estimation*. Wiley-Interscience, 1992. DOI: 10.1002/9780470316849. 18, 19, 20

Pierre Sermanet, David Eigen, Xiang Zhang, Michaël Mathieu, Rob Fergus, and Yann LeCun. Overfeat: Integrated recognition, localization and detection using convolutional networks. *arXiv preprint arXiv:1312.6229*, 2013. 5, 7

Yaser Sheikh and Mubarak Shah. Bayesian modeling of dynamic scenes for object detection. *IEEE Transaction on Pattern Analysis and Machine Intelligence*, 27:1778–1792, 2005. DOI: 10.1109/TPAMI.2005.213. 23

Yaser Sheikh, Omar Javed, and Takeo Kanade. Background Subtraction for Freely Moving Cameras. In *Proc. of the International Conference on Computer Vision*, 2009. DOI: 10.1109/ICCV.2009.5459334. 23, 46, 47, 48, 49, 50, 53, 54

Danijel Skocaj and Ales Leonardis. Weighted and robust incremental method for subspace learning. In *Proc. of the 9th International Conference on Computer Vision*, pages 1494–1501. IEEE, 2003. DOI: 10.1109/ICCV.2003.1238667. 25

Stefano Soatto, Gianfranco Doretto, and Ying Nian Wu. Dynamic textures. In *Proc. of the 8th International Conference on Computer Vision*, volume 2, pages 439–446, 2001. 23

Jürgen Stauder, Roland Mech, and Jörn Ostermann. Detection of moving cast shadows for object segmentation. *IEEE Transactions on Multimedia*, 1:65–76, 1999. DOI: 10.1109/6046.748172. 27

Chris Stauffer and W Eric L Grimson. Using adaptive tracking to classify and monitor activities in a site. In *Proc. of the IEEE Computer Society Conference on Computer Vision and Pattern Recognition*, 1998. DOI: 10.1109/CVPR.1998.698583. 16

Chris Stauffer and W Eric L Grimson. Adaptive background mixture models for real-time tracking. In *Proc. of the IEEE Computer Society Conference on Computer Vision and Pattern Recognition*, 1999. DOI: 10.1109/CVPR.1999.784637. 16, 17, 32

Bjoern Stenger, Visvanathan Ramesh, Nikos Paragios, Frans Coetzee, and Joachim M. Buhmann. Topology free hidden markov models: Application to background modeling. In *Proc. the 8th IEEE International Conference on Computer Vision*, 2001. DOI: 10.1109/ICCV.2001.937532. 24

Narayanan Sundaram, Thomas Brox, and Kurt Keutzer. Dense Point Trajectories by GPU-Accelerated Large Displacement Optical Flow. In *Proc. of the 11th European Conference on Computer Vision*, pages 438–451, 2010. DOI: 10.1007/978-3-642-15549-9_32. 44

Carlo Tomasi and Takeo Kanade. Shape and Motion from Image Streams under Orthography: a Factorization Method. *International Journal of Computer Vision*, 9(2):137–154, November 1992. ISSN 0920-5691. doi: 10.1007/BF00129684. http://www.springerlink.com/index/10.1007/BF00129684. DOI: 10.1007/BF00129684. 43

Philip HS Torr and Andrew Zisserman. Mlesac: A new robust estimator with application to estimating image geometry. *Computer Vision and Image Understanding*, 78(1):138–156, 2000. DOI: 10.1006/cviu.1999.0832. 39, 40

Philip H.S. Torr, Richard Szeliski, and P. Anandan. An Integrated Bayesian Approach to Layer Extraction from Image Sequences. *IEEE Transactions on Pattern Analysis and Machine Intelligence*, 23(3):297–303, 2001. DOI: 10.1109/34.910882. 46

Kentaro Toyama, John Krumm, Barry Brumitt, and Brian Meyers. Wallflower: Principles and practice of background maintenance. In *Proc. of the 7th IEEE International Conference on Computer Vision*, 1999. DOI: 10.1023/A:1008159011682. 10, 12, 23, 32, 34

Du-Ming Tsai and Shia-Chih Lai. Independent component analysis-based background subtraction for indoor surveillance. *IEEE Transactions on Image Processing*, 18(1):158–167, 2009. DOI: 10.1109/TIP.2008.2007558. 26

René Vidal and Richard I. Hartley. Motion segmentation with missing data using powerfactorization and GPCA. In *Proc. of the IEEE Computer Society Conference on Computer Vision and Pattern Recognition*, volume 2, pages 310–316, 2004. ISBN 0-7695-2158-4. doi: 10.1109/CVPR.2004.1315180. http://ieeexplore.ieee.org/lpdocs/epic03/wrapper.htm?arnumber=1315180. DOI: 10.1109/CVPR.2004.1315180. 43

Paul Viola and Michael J Jones. Robust real-time face detection. *International journal of computer vision*, 57(2):137–154, 2004. DOI: 10.1023/B:VISI.0000013087.49260.fb. 5

Toshikazu Wada and Takashi Matsuyama. Appearance sphere: Background model for pan-tilt-zoom camera. In *Proc. of the 13th International Conference on Pattern Recognition*, 1996. DOI: 10.1109/ICPR.1996.546118. 40

John Y.A. Wang and Edward H. Adelson. Representing Moving Images with Layers. *IEEE Transactions on Image Processing*, 2(5), 1994. DOI: 10.1109/83.334981. 44, 45

Jue Wang, Bo Thiesson, Yingqing Xu, and Michael Cohen. Image and Video Segmentation by Anisotropic Kernel Mean Shift. In *Proc. of the 4th European Conference on Computer Vision*, 2004. DOI: 10.1007/978-3-540-24671-8_19. 7

Lu Wang, Lei Wang, Ming Wen, Qing Zhuo, and Wenyuan Wang. Background subtraction using incremental subspace learning. In *Proc. of the IEEE International Conference on Image Processing*, pages V–45. IEEE, 2007. DOI: 10.1109/ICIP.2007.4379761. 25

Yair Weiss and Edward H. Adelson. A unified mixture framework for motion segmentation: incorporating spatial coherence and estimating the number of models. In *Proc. of the IEEE Computer Society Conference on Computer Vision and Pattern Recognition*, 1996. DOI: 10.1109/CVPR.1996.517092. 45

Christopher Richard Wern, Ali Azarbayejani, Trevor Darrell, and Alex Paul Pentland. Pfinder: Real-time tracking of human body. *IEEE Transaction on Pattern Analysis and Machine Intelligence*, 1997. DOI: 10.1109/34.598236. 10, 16

66 BIBLIOGRAPHY

Josh Wills, Sameer Agarwal, and Serge Belongie. What Went Where. In *Proc. of the IEEE Computer Society Conference on Computer Vision and Pattern Recognition*, 2003. DOI: 10.1109/CVPR.2003.1211335. 46

Masaki Yamazaki, Gang Xu, and Yen-Wei Chen. Detection of moving objects by independent component analysis. In *Proc. of the Asian Conference on Computer Vision*, pages 467–478. Springer, 2006. DOI: 10.1007/11612704_47. 26

Jingyu Yan and Marc Pollefeys. A General Framework for Motion Segmentation: Independent , Articulated, Rigid, Non-rigid, Degenerate and Non-degenerate. In *Proc. of the 9th European Conference on Computer Vision*, 2006. DOI: 10.1007/11744085_8. 43

Yee-Hong Yang and Martin D. Levine. The background primal sketch: An approach for tracking moving objects. *Machine Vision and Applications*, 5:17–34, 1992. DOI: 10.1007/BF01213527. 26

Wei Zhang, Xiang Zhong Fang, and Xiaokang Yang. Moving cast shadows detection based on ratio edge. In *Proc. of the International Conference on Pattern Recognition*, 2006. DOI: 10.1109/ICPR.2006.8187. 26, 31

Jing Zhong and Stan Sclaroff. Segmenting foreground objects from a dynamic textured background via a robust kalman filter. In *Proc. of the 9th IEEE International Conference on Computer Vision*, 2003. ISBN 0-7695-1950-4. DOI: 10.1109/ICCV.2003.1238312. 23

Author's Biography

AHMED ELGAMMAL

 **Dr. Elgammal** is an associate professor at the Department of Computer Science, Rutgers, the State University of New Jersey since Fall 2002. Dr. Elgammal is also a member of the Center for Computational Biomedicine Imaging and Modeling (CBIM). His primary research interest is computer vision and machine learning. His research focus includes human activity recognition, human motion analysis, tracking, human identification, and statistical methods for computer vision. Dr. Elgammal received the National Science Foundation CAREER Award in 2006. He has been the principal investigator and co-principal investigator of several research projects in the areas of human motion analysis, gait analysis, tracking, facial expression analysis and scene modeling; funded by NSF and ONR. Dr. Elgammal is a member of the review committee/board in several of the top conferences and journals in the computer vision field and is a senior IEEE member. Dr. Elgammal received his Ph.D. in 2002 and M.Sc. degree in 2000 in computer science from the University of Maryland, College Park. Dr. Elgammal received M.Sc. and B.E. degrees in computer science and automatic control from Alexandria University in 1996 and 1993, respectively.

Printed in the United States
by Baker & Taylor Publisher Services